The attack of four Seamen upon a party of Sepoys at Arrorha.

THE CRUISE OF THE PEARL

WITH AN ACCOUNT OF THE OPERATIONS

OF THE

NAVAL BRIGADE IN INDIA
1857-1858

REV. E. A. WILLIAMS, MA,
CHAPLAIN, ROYAL NAVY

The Naval & Military Press Ltd

published in association with

FIREPOWER
The Royal Artillery Museum
Woolwich

Published by
The Naval & Military Press Ltd
Unit 10 Ridgewood Industrial Park,
Uckfield, East Sussex,
TN22 5QE England
Tel: +44 (0) 1825 749494
Fax: +44 (0) 1825 765701
www.naval-military-press.com

in association with

FIREPOWER
The Royal Artillery Museum, Woolwich
www.firepower.org.uk

In reprinting in facsimile from the original, any imperfections are inevitably reproduced and the quality may fall short of modern type and cartographic standards.

ADVERTISEMENT.

To the Reader.

The following Narrative is selected from a Journal which was originally written without the slightest intention of committing it to the press; but, on the representation of several friends, I have ventured to publish that portion of it which treats chiefly of the services of the "Pearl's" Naval Brigade in India, and which I thought would be interesting to the public; and trust that the truth of the statements may so far conciliate the opinion of the reader, that he will forgive its other deficiences.

E. A. Williams,
Chaplain, Royal Navy.

July 22nd, 1859.

INTRODUCTION.

The only excuse I can offer for publishing the following brief and imperfect Narrative is, that it gives an account of the services of seamen on shore of an unprecedented character. This is, I believe, the only example in English history of officers and seamen of the Royal Navy leaving their ships, and taking their guns seven or eight hundred miles into the interior of a great continent, to serve as soldiers, marching and counter-marching for fifteen months through extensive districts, and taking an active part in upwards of twenty actions. I have refrained from making any remarks on the services of the Naval Brigade of H.M. ship "Shannon," with which I had not an opportunity of being sufficiently acquainted. But the events I have endeavoured to depict with reference to the Naval Brigade of H.M. ship "Pearl," to which I was attached as Chaplain during the two harassing and trying campaigns of 1857 and 1858, I have had ample opportunity of knowing, either from personal observation, or the statements of those on whose veracity I can rely.

Although the Narrative does not tell of thousands slain in battle, or describe the shaking of nations under the crash of contending armies, it nevertheless embodies an account of services rendered to the State, great, when compared with the means employed. The country acknowledged these services in the thanks of both Houses of Parliament having been passed to the Royal Navy and Royal Marines as well as to the army; and Sir Michael Seymour, the Naval Commander-in-Chief, expressed his high approbation of the gallantry and good conduct of the Naval Brigades. "Their services," he remarked, "won the distinguished approval of Her Most Gracious Majesty and the Lords Commissioners of the Admiralty," and their "brilliant campaign he had viewed with pride," feeling "that the honours so gallantly won by the Naval Brigades in India are reflected upon the Navy at large."

The opinion of one so deserving of respect, gives me reason to suppose that a Narrative of what was done by them in the Upper Provinces of India may prove acceptable to the public. It is not that more credit can be claimed for this small force than for any other equal number of Britons under similar circumstances; but it is considerations arising from the difficulties that were overcome, the isolated position that was occupied, totally unsupported by Europeans, for many months; the holding of an advanced post exposed to constant attacks, and removed from the rest of the army so far that its services and dangers have been little known, that afford an additional excuse for describing the part taken by the Royal Navy, and which may fill up a hitherto vacant niche in Indian history; and adding as it did to the strength of the army in Artillery when troops were few, and that arm of the service in particular was loudly called for in the country, I hope the following Narrative may show how it contributed a *quota* towards the many triumphs in India which shed lustre on the British arms.

LONDON, *July 22nd*, 1859.

CONTENTS.

CHAPTER I.

Armament of H.M.S. "Pearl"—Voyage to Madeira—Rio de Janeiro—Straits of Magellan—Peruvian Revolutions—Capture of the "Loa" and "Tumbes"—Attack of the "Apurimac" on the forts of Callao . . . . pp. 1—32

CHAPTER II.

Voyage to the Sandwich Islands—Honolulu—State of Education—Knowledge and Practice of Medicine by the Natives—The Valley and Missionary Station of Kaneohe—Voyage to China—Boat expedition against Chinese Pirates—Orders to sail for India—Arrival at Calcutta . . . . 33—56

CHAPTER III.

Royal Marines garrison Fort William—The Mohurrum at Calcutta—Naval Brigade embarked in the "Chunar"—Quarters in Buxar—Naval Brigade at Chupra—Camp at Myrwa—The Attack on Goothnee—The Rebels advance to Sohunpore—The first Alarm . . . . 57—80

CHAPTER IV.

Arrival of a Gorkha Regiment—Gorkha Arms—Action at Sohunpore—Flight of the Enemy—Their Camp taken—Sarun saved—Activity of Seamen in the management of Horses—All difficulties overcome—Defenceless State of the Country—Advantages of this Victory—Advance on Roodurpore—Punishment of Rebels pp. 81—107

CHAPTER V.

The Fleet of Boats proceed up the Gogra—Captain Sotheby in Command of the Escort—Perilous Nature of the Expedition—Taking of the Fort of Chanderpore—The Crossing of the Gogra—Battle of Phoolpore—Gun turned upon the Enemy by the Royal Marines—A Kookrie Charge—Naval Brigade recross the Gogra—Prejudices of the Gorkhas regarding the Slaying of the Ox,
108—135

CHAPTER VI.

Jung Bahadoor's Durbar—Nepalese Uniform—March to Kuptangunge—Character of the Country—The Fort of Belwa—The Bengal Yeomanry Cavalry join our Force—The Attack on Belwa . 136—148

CHAPTER VII.

The Country disaffected—Perilous Position of the Field Force—Destruction of a Village by Elephants—Battle of Amorha—Disparity of Numbers—Rout of the Enemy—Goruckpore saved—Sikhs looting Propensity . . . . 149—174

CHAPTER VIII.

Constant Alarms—A Fort constructed—The Rebels Reinforced—Arrival of the left Wing of H.M. 13th Light Infantry—The Hot Season—Camp Routine —Action near Tilga—Charge of the Bengal Yeomanry Cavalry—The Westerly Winds, pp. 175—196.

CHAPTER IX.

Action near Jamoulee—Captain Clarke's attack on the Rebels near Bustee—Fatiguing March from Amorha—Taking of Nuggur—Bustee saved, 197—212

CHAPTER X.

The Nepalese Army on its return Home—Government Servants mutilated—The Men lodged in Huts—A Locomotive Library—Recreation for the Men—Alarms—The First of the Dours—Attack on the Ranee's House at Amorha—The Rebels beaten at Hurreah . . . . 213—234

CHAPTER XI.

Engagement with the Rebels near Lumptee—Attack on Hurreah—The Rebels beaten at Debreah— Dour to Bansee—Harassing March—The Rebels beaten at Doomureahgunge—Second Dour to Bansee—The Enemy beaten at Amorha—Jugdespore attacked—Rebels routed at Doomureahgunge —Rebels attacked at Bururiah . . . 235—260

CHAPTER XII.

The Rebels enclosed in a Net—The Force encamped at Intwa—Obedience of Elephants—The Force marches into Oudh—Battle of Toolseepore—The Siege Train—The Town of Toolseepore after the Battle . . . . pp. 261—281

CHAPTER XIII.

Christmas Day, 1858—March to Pepyreah—Sir Hope Grant's Flying Column—March to Puchpurwah—Naval Brigade ordered to the Ship—The Farewell—Governor-General's Opinion of the Naval Brigade—Dinner given to the Seamen at Calcutta—Dinner given to the Officers at Madras—Voyage Home—Names of Officers . . . . . 282—311

THE CRUISE OF THE PEARL

ROUND THE WORLD.

CHAPTER I.

Armament of H.M.S. "Pearl"—Voyage to Madeira—Rio de Janeiro—Straits of Magellan—Peruvian Revolutions—Capture of the "Loa" and "Tumbes"—Attack of the "Apurimac" on the forts of Callao.

On the 24th of December, 1855, H.M.'s screw steam-ship "Pearl" was commissioned by Captain Sotheby, R.N., at Woolwich. When ready for sea, she proceeded to Portsmouth, where it was intended she should join the fleet which was assembling for the third expedition to the Baltic.

The "Pearl" was the first of the new class of 21-gun corvettes, which had been commissioned. Her armament consisted of

8-inch guns, having one 95-cwt. pivot-gun; and, considering her tonnage, draught of water, weight of metal, and steam power, she was regarded as a most effective ship, and well suited to the Baltic, and, consequently, likely to see much active service. For these reasons the command of her would naturally present more attractions to an enterprising officer than a line-of-battle ship, which would in all probability spend most of her time at anchor.

In the spring of 1856 she went to sea for a fortnight on a trial trip, and, after encountering a severe gale, returned to Spithead without suffering any damage, and proving herself to be an admirable sea-boat.

The Russian war being now over, peace was proclaimed; and as there was no prospect of a Baltic expedition, the "Pearl" was got ready for a foreign station. With the utmost speed she was fitted out for a long voyage, and, when ready for foreign service, was ordered to sail for the South American and Pacific station.

We left Spithead on the 30th day of May, 1856, steamed through the Needles, and bid farewell to the shores of old England, not knowing what changes would take place, what scenes we were destined to witness, or what service was destined to await us between that day and the date of our return. On the following day we called in at Plymouth, and in the afternoon were again at sea.

On the 9th of June we arrived at Madeira, where a few days were pleasantly spent. There were two American men-of-war at anchor at Funchal, the "James Town" and "St. Lewis;" the former, a corvette, was the Commodore's flag-ship; the latter was a smaller vessel which accompanied the Commodore. Their station was the West Coast of Africa, and they had come from thence to spend the summer months at Madeira, and thus, by avoiding the intolerable heat of an African sun, they wisely discovered a very agreeable method of passing away a commission on "the Coast." At this time the feeling between England and the United States was not very amicable, and at first some doubts existed as to who should take the initiative in the formulæ of civilities. However, the ice was soon broken, and the best of goodwill soon prevailed.

The United States' Consul invited the officers of the "Pearl" to a ball, and their Transatlantic friends lost no time in inviting them to "liquor." One would begin, "I say, stranger, will you liquor?" In the first place, the health of the Queen, for whom they entertain the greatest respect, would be loyally proposed. This would be quickly followed by the health of the President and Congress; then he would propose the health of themselves; next, the health of the Crimean heroes; then, if he could not think of any one else, he would propose the health of the Queen again. This process being perpetually repeated, health after health following each other in quick succession, so that, when taken by storm with this kind of Transatlantic friendship, it required some firmness of purpose to avoid the natural consequences. At any rate, whatever disputes disturb cabinets, it is quite clear that there is in the navy a happy knack of settling them by a glass of Madeira, as well as by stronger measures.

On the 13th of June we weighed anchor and left Madeira, proceeding on our voyage towards Rio de Janeiro. The morning was fine, and the wind was fair when we left behind us the narrow dirty streets of Funchal. At this time, however, it was unusually clean. The Royal yacht having lately arrived there on a cruise, gave rise to a vague rumour that the Queen would visit the island during the summer; and in consequence of this report, by a general order of the Governor, the houses were whitewashed and appeared in a new dress. The scenery, the work of nature, presents a pleasing contrast with the town, the work of man. The lofty mountains and sunny valleys, where the rose, the pink, and geranium grow wild, and where the fuchsia and the fern flourish in harmony together, are a great relief to the eye of the traveller when he emerges from the narrow, toasting, grilling pavements of Funchal.

July 12th. We anchored in the magnificent harbour of Rio de Janeiro. It is supposed to be unequalled by any harbour in the world except that at Sydney. The scenery is exceedingly picturesque. The entrance is not much more than a quarter of a mile wide, and protected by a strong fort; and, after entering, it opens out into a splendid haven surrounded by mountains. In the distance, at the further side, the

Organ mountains rise majestically, and add all the beauty that hill and forest can give to a beautiful sheet of water studded with picturesque islands. St. Sebastian is situated on the south side of the harbour, and is the chief city in the empire of Brazil. It is much improved of late years, and gives evidence of being the seat of government of a rising kingdom. Since their declaration of independence in 1822, great strides have been made, trade has increased, and education has been promoted.

In a beautiful valley near the summit of the Organ mountains,* is a sanitarium for the people of St. Sebastian. It is named Petropolis, after Peter the Second, Emperor of Brazil. The colony is chiefly inhabited by Germans, with a mixture of French, English, and Brazilians. Here the Emperor has a country palace, where he can retire when the heat of the plains becomes excessive.

---

* Or Terra San Salvador.

The system of locomotion from the capital to Petropolis is made as easy and convenient as possible: a steamer conveys passengers to the upper end of the harbour; from thence to the foot of the mountains they are conveyed by a railway; and from the railway terminus to Petropolis, the means of conveyance is by a small carriage, drawn by four mules at a canter, up a well-made macadamized road—the ascent being regular and gentle from the bottom to the top, a height of about two thousand five hundred feet. The road is about ten miles long, and is a splendid piece of engineering; it winds through the deep indents, and round the spurs of the mountains, presenting at every turn a new and varied prospect. Education also seems to be the object of the chief care of the Government. Here two excellent colleges for boys are established, and a seminary for young ladies, in addition to numerous schools for the lower classes.

The population seems industrious and prosperous; their cottages are neat and clean; and crime is rare among them. The climate is as tolerable as can be expected on the borders of the tropics; and on the whole, there is the appearance of a thriving colony, and the advantage of a cool retreat to the merchants of the capital during the heat of the summer months.

July 22nd. Left Rio harbour, and, sailing southward, on the 8th of August entered the Straits of Magellan. At eight o'clock the same evening we anchored off Cape Possession, on the coast of Patagonia. Each morning early the steam was got up and we were under weigh by daylight; and every evening at dusk we came to an anchor. The water was as smooth as a millpond. We were fortunate in meeting neither fogs nor gales of wind; and on the 13th, after four days, we emerged from the straits into the Pacific Ocean, and thus succeeded in cheating Cape Horn of the accustomed homage which ships usually pay in pitching and rolling in an unmerciful manner. We stopped for half a day at Sandy Point, where the Chilians have a military settlement; and we stopped a day at Fortescue Bay, when, the weather being threatening, it might have been dangerous to pass through the narrow channels.

The climate was by no means so cold as we expected to find it at this season of the year. The mountains were covered with snow, but it did not reach down to the water; and a great coat was as much additional clothing as was required. The Chilian settlement at Sandy Point was formed after the mutiny which broke out at Port Famine about four years previously, when the governor was killed, and the convicts were let loose; some of whom were afterwards executed at Valparaiso.

From the entrance of the straits up to

this place, the land on both sides is rather flat and uninteresting, being only occasionally varied by a precipitous cliff or bluff headland, or a hill some distance in the interior; but from this place until the waters of the straits mingle with the vast expanse of the Pacific Ocean, the mountains rise from the water's edge, sometimes abruptly, sometimes gradually, covered with trees and verdure, until the trees and verdure in their turn are covered with snow. Sailing along, we observed in the clefts of the mountains several beautiful glaciers of a light azure tint which seemed like some mighty torrent arrested in its course, and frozen into rocks of ice before it had time to fall. The straits vary from a mile and a half in the narrows to five-and-twenty or thirty miles wide, and are upwards of three hundred miles in length. The population is scanty, and those who are seen along the shores seem to be about the lowest in the scale of uncivilization, living little better than the wild beasts of the forest, their food rancid fish or seals; and inhabiting hovels or wigwams made of the branches of trees, which do not exhibit so much ingenuity in their construction as that of the ant or the birds of the air; while the country through which they roam, untutored and ungoverned, is most picturesque in its features, splendid in the barren magnificence of its cliffs and mountains, and strikingly majestic in the bold headlands dipping down almost perpendicularly into the sea. Having left the Straits of Magellan on the 13th August, we arrived at Valparaiso at the end of the same month. The "Pearl" then continued on the Pacific station, for which she was originally intended, until the 5th of April, 1857. She touched at various ports on the coasts of South and Central America; but during this time nothing of importance occurred beyond what usually occurs to most men-of-war, except the capture of two Peruvian gunboats, which took place on the 28th of March, a few days before leaving the station—a punishment which they brought down upon themselves by committing an outrage on the English flag.

The government of Peru was at this time, as usual, what might be called remarkably "shaky." Revolutions in small republics on the coast of America are of ordinary occurrence, and in Peru the number of general officers is so great compared with the rest of the army, that they very often find themselves out of employment, and, for the want of anything better to do, set up a claim to be President of the republic; but, in order to obtain this enviable appointment, it is necessary to oust the reigning President. To effect this object he is not attacked in the Congress on the ground of misgovernment, and got rid of by the opinion of the country; but they appeal to arms !—a revolution is stirred up, and as many adherents are collected together as have not had any share in the government offices or appointments for some time previously, and who are of opinion that they have as good or a better right to administer justice as well as expend the public treasury as those already in power. It is never very difficult for a clever adventurer, or rather patriot, to collect around his standard a cloud of these wronged and neglected heroes, who are ready to fight for a due share in the administration, or die in the attempt. It was during one of these patriotic struggles that our lot was cast in Callao Roads, when General Castillia being President of Peru, Señor Vivanco considered that he was not the right man in such a place. General Castillia was a brave old soldier who never shrunk from danger, who won the President's seat by the sword, and was resolved to retain it by the same. He had the sympathy of the army and the mass of the people on his side, while Señor Vivanco had the sympathy of the higher classes, but more particularly of the ladies, who exercise a great influence in the politics of Peru. The naval force was not quite equally divided, the greater portion of their navy upholding the cause of Vivanco, while only a few took the side of Castillia. Such was the condition of the country when one fine evening (Tuesday, the 24th March, 1857) a soirée was given by the officers on board H.M.S. " Pearl," to which many of the inhabitants of Lima and Callao were invited. During the entertainment, intelligence arrived that two small war-steamers, whose officers and crews had espoused the cause of Vivanco, stopped our mail-steamer, the "New Grenada," on her way to Panamá, and having boarded her, placed sentries in different parts of the ship, searched her, and abstracted thirty-two thousand dollars, besides bales of goods and articles of less value which had been shipped under the names of merchants at Valparaiso, but in reality had been sent up by Castillia to pay his troops in the northern part of the country.

According to orders given by Admiral Bruce, we weighed anchor next day about noon, and sailed northward in search of the "Loa" and "Tumbes," which were the two vessels that had committed the outrage on the English flag.

On the 28th March we arrived at Lambeyaque, where the "New Grenada" had been plundered, and where it was expected the vessels would be lying at anchor. It was so arranged by Captain Sotheby that we should arrive by daybreak, and take them by surprise. About six o'clock in the morning ships were seen ahead, and as it was impossible to tell but that resistance might be made, the bugle sounded to general quarters, and the "Pearl" was ready for action. On nearing the ships, the "Loa" and "Tumbes" were recognised; and all hands on board seemed to be at general quarters also. Coming upon them in the grey dawn, they at first mistook the "Pearl" for the "Apurimac" (44 guns), which was the flag-ship of Vivanco's fleet, and the officers in command were in full dress ready to pay their respects to their admiral, until the English ensign being hoisted at the peak, as the "Pearl" steamed up alongside, dispelled the illusion, and the unpleasant truth became apparent that a foe instead of a friend was approaching. Our boats having been manned and armed, Mr. Turmour, the First Lieutenant of the "Pearl," went on board the "Loa," which was the senior officer's ship, and demanded the 32,000 dollars and bales of goods which had been abstracted, and also the officers and men who had committed the outrage; and in default of the fulfilment of these terms, in five minutes, an immediate surrender. It was impossible to comply with the first of these terms, as the cash had been distributed among Vivanco's needy dependents as soon as it was captured. The Captain, in consequence, came on board the "Pearl" and surrendered, offering to give up his sword, which was refused, as it was not the object of the expedition to capture them as enemies' ships, but simply to inflict punishment for a predatory excursion, and keep them as hostages until they could inspire hopes of their better behaviour for the future. The Captain of the "Tumbes" followed the example of his senior officer.

The officers and men who had taken no part in the affair of the New Granada had their option to go ashore at Lambeyaque or proceed to Callao. The latter they preferred, being desirous to remain with their companions and await the issue of the matter. Lieutenant Radcliffe was ordered to take charge of the "Loa," with a few of the

"Pearl's" crew as a guard; some of her own officers and men being left on board to assist in working the ship, while Lieutenant Grant took charge of the "Tumbes" with another party of men, to conduct them back to Callao, there to await the investigation of the affair, and the decision of the Commander-in-Chief of the station. The "Loa" and "Tumbes" were two fine gun boats, built in England for the Peruvian Government, the former carrying four guns (long 32-pounders) and the latter two guns of the same calibre, each having one brass gun in addition.

Some of the crews of the gunboats having been drafted on board the "Pearl," and some of the "Pearl's" men having been sent to them in exchange as a guard, while a sufficient number of their own crews were left on board to do the rough work, including their engineers, who were Englishmen, we left on the same afternoon, and steamed back towards Callao with one gunboat on each quarter. Nothing of any importance took place on our return except the inconvenience of having so many additional hands on board. It was, however, quite clear from all that could be made out of the conflicting statements of the officers that they had used unpardonable violence, some of them acknowledged much that others, wishing to shield themselves from blame, were very vehement in denying; and he who had been the principal actor in the affair, and had placed the sentries in the ships when the dollars were abstracted, we were afterwards informed had been originally an owner of a cart which conveyed goods from Callao to Lima, and subsequently had been promoted to be a master of a trading vessel on the coast, and finally attained the rank of an officer in the Peruvian navy. Under these circumstances it could scarcely be expected that he should have known much of the law of nations.

One incident, however, produced a little excitement. Late in the evening a light was seen ahead. It was conjectured that the admiral on board the "Apurimac" might have had tidings of the pursuit, and was coming to their assistance; there was a rumour that she had sailed northward, and this strengthened the conjecture. The bugle sounded to general quarters, and precautions were taken against a surprise. The Peruvian officers were puzzled, not knowing what to think of it. In the countenance of some, consternation was depicted, some affected indifference to the rumour. But among all for several minutes there was a breathless silence. Certainly, it must be acknowledged that if an attempt had been made to cut out the ships it would have been very unsatisfactory to those Peruvians on board the "Pearl" to be made a target for the shot and shell of one of their own ships which came to their rescue. The suspense, however, did not last long; the light a-head soon disappeared, a retreat was sounded and the excitement subsided.

On the 31st of March, having returned to Callao with the two vessels, great excitement was produced among the inhabitants. The beach was lined with spectators to witness the return of the "Loa" and the "Tumbes;" they were exceedingly wroth, and expressed their indignation in no measured terms, at their ships having been brought in, as they said, like pirates, without their flags flying; and the "Pearl," which had been previously tolerably popular, suddenly sunk in general estimation. One of the vessels was given up to the party from whom she had been taken, and the other was kept for some time as a security that such a depredation should not be committed again.

Castillia had offered a large reward of several thousand pounds for the capture of these two steamers, which, no doubt, would have been promptly paid if they had been delivered up to him; but as it was not the intention of England to take an active part in the support of either party, they were therefore not given up to him; in the mean time, however, he took advantage of the blunder made by his opponent, and the consequent embarrassment that his blunder entailed, by sending troops to the north to attack Vivanco's forces. The Peruvian soldiers, most of whom are Cholos, that is, the original natives of the country, chiefly from the hills, are a strong hardy race of men; they are for the most part of low stature and swarthy complexion, their limbs are thick and their shoulders broad; they are capable of enduring much fatigue, and making very long marches. There is a plant called the "Coca," the leaves of which they chew, much in the same way as tobacco is used by some Europeans, but its effects are very different. It is said that the soldier of Peru will go a great number of hours without food if he has the coca leaf to chew, which seems to soothe, and dispel the feeling of hunger, and although it is so great a stimulant, it leaves no bad effects behind. Under its influence they undergo much fatigue, and march surprising distances with the greatest cheerfulness and endurance.

It is by these intestine feuds that Peru is becoming gradually depopulated, and its once fertile provinces are rapidly falling into desolate wastes. In these revolutions brother rises against brother, and father against son; the ties of kindred seem to be no barrier to the shedding of blood. In fact, there is a certain policy in the members of the same family adopting opposite politics, this plan sometimes works with advantage to the parties concerned. When one side gains the day, the victor generally has interest enough to secure the pardon of the offending brother; his point has been gained, he has got into power, and is in a fair way of making a competent fortune. When party feeling has subsided he no longer thirsts for his brother's blood; natural feelings take their proper place and assume their rightful prerogative, and he is reprieved. Such a state of things is ruinous to the country; the thinking portion of the community regret it, while they are too few to have weight enough to reform it. Morally, physically, and socially, the contrast this country presents with the account we have of it under its former sovereigns, the Incas, is most striking. Prosperity has never attended the footsteps of the conquerors. The first stone of their power was laid in a thirst for gold which was gained by injustice, treachery, and blood—that thirst has never been slaked. No settled, well organized Government remains as an evidence of the power, wisdom, and sagacity of the victors, the inhabitants are rapidly diminishing in numbers, and the lands show no signs of fertility. The depopulation which has been going on for years may be attributed to various causes. From many millions at the time of the conquest they have dwindled down to about three millions, or a little more. This may be attributed to the bad government which has existed, to the tyranny which has been practised, and to the civil wars and riots which have perpetually prevailed, as well as to diseases which have been introduced without medical men in sufficient numbers throughout the country to apply remedies, and to many other causes. Added to which, a constant series of revolutions which have followed each other in rapid succession, as one wave follows another, has disturbed the country for years.

A president is elected for five years, but before three years have run their course, some unhorsed, hungry general raises a party to put him out. This struggle, which is tantamount to a change of ministry among other nations, lasts, perhaps, for a year or two, when one or other conquers, and is put out in his turn by some other aspiring competitor. Wise heads make a mercantile speculation out of these revolutions; they lend money at a high interest to the contending parties. Whoever attains office pays handsomely, while the defeated are sometimes not only beggared, but beggar their friends and supporters also. They all sink or swim in the same boat, their contentions do not seem to be even tinged with patriotism. Their disregard for life is great, they hold it cheap. Their insatiable thirst for gold has descended through the line of their Spanish ancestors, but their energy, enterprise, and chivalry have formed no part of the inheritance. Travelling in the country is neither very safe nor convenient, and so weak is the Government that the most dangerous roads in the empire are those within ten miles of Lima, the principal city, where the traveller would expect to find the police the most efficient. In that neighbourhood, if alone, he is more in danger of being robbed and plundered by assassins and gangs of liberated negroes than in any other part of the country.

Of the ladies I have little to say, except that they are usually seen by candlelight, when they appear pleasing and good looking. Their figure is graceful, and their manners easy and affable. It is not the custom to visit during the day, except on Sundays or holidays; but in the evening their reception rooms, which, in Lima, are the first apartments on entering the house, (no hall leading from the door to the drawing room as in England,) is illuminated by many lights; and if not lit up, with the ladies dressed as if for an evening party, it is evident to the visitor that the inmates do not intend to receive visits that evening, or are gone to spend the evening with some other friends. Their greatest expenditure seems to be on the furniture of their reception rooms, and their dress; on these they spare no expense. They have no carriages, because they have no roads to drive them on. The men use riding horses when going a long distance, but the ladies are too fond of the *dolce far niente* to appreciate such violent exercise.

The Peruvian navy did not seem to be so often called into action as the army in their late revolutionary movements. This may have arisen partly from the fact that the greater number of the ships were in the hands of Vivanco. The only one that Castillia possessed which was a match for the "Apurimac" being the "Amazon," which had been abroad for several months. Report said that Castillia avoided the risk of a naval engagement, not having confidence that the officers and crews would be true to his standard. Once only while the "Pearl" was lying in Callao Roads, there was an attack made by the frigate "Apurimac" on the forts at Callao, and a small steamer called the "Ucayali," with the intention, if possible, of cutting her out. The "Ucayali" was close in-shore, alongside the mole, or pier, on which several guns were mounted. The Peruvian admiral conceived a plan of surprising this vessel, expecting to sink her if he could not succeed in her capture. Just before the dawn of day one misty morning she steamed stealthily close up to the mole where she was anchored, and delivered a broadside; so well was the surprise conducted, that the first intimation given of her approach was a shot through the surgeon's cabin, which aroused him from his peaceful slumbers; consequently there was ample time to discharge several rounds of shot and grape before the fire was returned. The fight then lasted about half an hour—it was hot work on both sides. Spectators in the different merchant ships were aroused by the booming of the cannon. The gunnery of both parties was not calculated to inspire any one with fear except those who had nothing to do with the affair. From the fort and the mole many shots were fired, but few took effect, considering the close proximity of the belligerents. Several men, however, were wounded, and three or four were killed. A request was sent to the surgeon of the "Pearl" to lend his aid, which was at once complied with. Most of the shots fired at the "Ucayali" were too high, they did not calculate on such close quarters. If the gunnery practice had been as good as the manner in which the vessel was brought into position, and if the manœuvre had been carried out as well as it was planned, it would have met with better success. But so high was the elevation of the guns that many of the shot went over the houses in the town, carrying terror into the homes of peaceful citizens, and causing them to fly in alarm and dismay along the road which led to Lima. Among other casualties, it was reported that a child was killed in the arms of its mother, which she afterwards carried to the President, no doubt to excite his commiseration, and to show what misery these civil feuds entail.

CHAPTER II.

Voyage to the Sandwich Islands—Honolulu—State of Education—Knowledge and Practice of Medicine by the Natives—The Valley and Missionary Station of Kaneohe—Voyage to China—Boat Expedition against Chinese Pirates—Orders to sail for India—Arrival at Calcutta.

IN the afternoon of the 5th of April we weighed anchor and left Callao Roads, on a long voyage across the Pacific to China. Having fair winds and fine weather, we arrived at the Sandwich Islands on the 9th of May, and on the morning of the 10th steamed into the harbour of Honolulu. This city, containing five or six thousand inhabitants, is situated on the Island Oahu. Some of the houses are built of wood and some are of stone, so that, it presents the appearance in its architecture of an American rather than a European city: Americans and American interests also predominate. The King of this group of islands, of which Honolulu is the chief city, is Kamehameha the Fourth. He is an intelligent man and very much in advance of his predecessor. Both himself and his Queen Emma, who is partly of European extraction, seem to be popular among their people.

The population of the Sandwich Islands, which is about 75,000 or 80,000, is now in a very different condition from what it was thirty years ago, the inhabitants, from having been wild and uncivilized, are now all nominally Christians. It has been stated that when they use an oath, it is in the English language, having no words to that effect in their own. What a slur on a people, civilized, and professing a pure Christianity! Much credit is due to the American missionaries, who have worked with energy and zeal for many years, and much success has attended their labours. The Kanakas* are simple-minded and docile, but being naturally idle and immoral, are often more easily led astray by the allurements of vice offered to them by Americans and Europeans who do not feel the restraints of religion, than persuaded to follow the path of virtue by those who labour among them for that object. One of the missionaries gave it as his opinion that the boys go onward and upward under the influence of education, while the girls go backward and downward in sin and vice, and if other means and fresh appliances are not used to arrest this great evil, the prospect for the future generations is sad indeed. This statement, however, applied chiefly to the Island of Oahu, where foreigners are numerous. The population of the rural districts in the other islands is on the increase, while

---

* This word means, in the Hawaiian language, "man," and is used to express "native of the islands."

in the seaport towns, where vice prevails, it is diminishing.

They have several large churches in Honolulu, and the congregations are as numerous and attentive as in any English church. Each missionary station has now settled down, and assumes the character of a parochial charge rather than a missionary settlement. Some years ago the parent missionary society in the United States resolved to reduce the expenses, which had been considerably on the increase, and accordingly proposed to contribute a certain reduced amount, and that the rest should be raised by the native congregations or other means; and if the missionaries found it impossible to carry on the work with the reduced allowances, the board was ready to defray their expenses home again. Most of them, however, remained. A large sum is subscribed annually by the native congregations who can afford it towards the stipend of the pastor and the support of the church. The work went on as usual, and the expenses of the home society were considerably diminished. One congregation in Honolulu contributes upwards of 600 dollars or 120*l.* annually towards the stipend of the pastor; and although the Hawaiians are naturally selfish, yet when Christian principle takes root, they have afforded many examples of generosity.

If we were to judge from the number of schools in the island, and from the law of the land which obliges children between the age of four and fourteen to attend, we should be led to suppose that education was flourishing. The teachers certainly seemed to attend to their work; but the materials, as may be expected with all races which have recently emerged from barbarism, are not the most promising to work upon. The race has not yet received the culture and training of centuries, and therefore the minds of the young do not possess that grasp and capacity which is found among European nations. The children are quick in picking up some things until they arrive at a certain point; but to urge them one step in advance requires a considerable effort, both on the part of the teacher and the taught. The rudiments, such as reading, writing, geography, and arithmetic, are easily acquired, but it is difficult to get them much further. Their memory is good—it seems to be their best faculty—but few give evidence of a high order of intellect; time, patience, and perseverance, have, however, done much, and, no doubt, will produce greater fruit in future. The present race of teachers have been their instructors for many years, and as the system of instruction varies and improves in the process of time, like most other things in this age of progress, it might not be amiss if fresh blood was introduced in that department.

In one or two of the schools there is a great mixture of races. You might see English, Irish, American, and some half-caste boys as well as natives. I have also seen the children of a Tahitian and a North American Indian. Under these circumstances it would be productive of much good to introduce the English language more than it has yet been done, and which, if energetically attempted, many of the apparent obstacles would vanish. Some years ago it might easily have been done; their own language containing so few words, it was found necessary to coin a multitude of others to express and describe various new things which were introduced. If these things had simply been called by the English name, the language might almost insensibly have been introduced.

The children in the schools are much gratified at being noticed by visitors, and are vociferous in their "aloha," meaning

" peace," which is their method of salutation, and is suitable either to a meeting or parting. Their complexion ascends, through various degrees, from a light copper colour to a shade nearly black. Their dark bright eyes, when their fuzzy black hair is combed off their brows, present a tolerably intellectual spark. I observed that when one of the boys, in reading English, came to a word which he did not know how to pronounce, he miscalled it, and tacked on an "*s*" to the end, supposing that he could thereby manufacture an English word. This seems to be a common habit. The mottoes suspended in some of the schools are truly characteristic of the States, of which the following is an example:—

" Be sure you are right,

Go a-head."

The male population are a good height, athletic, and well proportioned; but neither men nor women are prepossessing in appearance, although they have the reputation of being good-tempered and not easily aroused into anger.

The ruins of an old temple are still to be seen about six miles from Honolulu, near Diamond Hill. It is said to have been built by Kamehameha the First, after the conquest of the island. It is called Heiau. Here, in the days of heathenism, were offered human sacrifices. The victim was chosen either by the priest or king. The messenger of death entered his abode while he slept, and he met his end by strangling. He was then dragged off as an offering to the sanguinary god. Some affirm that the priests ate the flesh of the victim, but for this there is but little foundation; and it is now thought that the people in general never were cannibals.

Although the light of truth has dispelled much of the mist of ignorance and error, there are, however, still some of their former superstitions deeply rooted among them. In the healing art they are sometimes absurdly apparent. Their native doctors have recourse to charms and incantations in preference to medicine, of which they are totally ignorant. These learned sons of Æsculapius will put a row of charmed stones about the diseased part of the body which is to be cured, and walk round, uttering screams and yells, and making strange grotesque grimaces in order to restore the sick to health.

One of these distinguished practitioners found himself incarcerated one day in consequence of one of his unsuccessful experiments terminating in the death of the patient, a catastrophe which could not by any possibility be brought in *secundum artem*. He had been called in to try his skill on a man who was deranged. The sufferer had, although unintentionally, been partly the innocent cause of the death of another man by drowning. Subsequently (probably by the accident preying on his mind), he became deranged. The doctor having duly considered the case, and thoroughly investigated the cause of the disease, prescribed that he should be cured by water. The water-cure was forthwith resorted to. With the assistance of four strong men (his wife and friends consenting, and being fully convinced of the efficacy of the cure), he was bound hand and foot, and then tied down with the water up to his chin. The men who were stationed to watch him, and who ought to have observed the progress of the cure, lay down and fell asleep. When they awoke the man was drowned. The doctor and his accomplices were of course taken up and tried. The wife of the deceased was so fully convinced that the treatment was correct, although it unfortunately failed in this case, that she made every effort to procure the acquittal of the culprit. She again had recourse to another doctor, who supplied her with pills, which she was to take when the case came on in court, and by means of which the jury were to be so spell-bound as to give a verdict in his favour. The case came on; law was more potent than charms. The four accomplices escaped on the ground that they were hired servants of the doctor, but the doctor himself was safely lodged in jail. There is another superstition prevalent among the lower class. They fancy that some men are gifted with the power to pray their enemy to death. It sometimes occurs that if a man has a quarrel with his neighbour who happens to obtain one of his garments, the man who lost his garment would be in a great state of alarm lest the other got possession of it in order to have a spell or charm over him. And very often the fear of their enemy praying them to death so works on their imagination as to produce the effect.

They do not believe themselves endowed with the power of praying a white man to death. They have had a practical example of their impotency in this matter. It was once tried on John Young, who had been a boatswain in the American ship "Eleanor." He was detained on the island in consequence of the taboo having been laid on the canoes, which were not allowed to leave the shore. The ship put to sea without him, and on finding himself a resident on the island, he married a native lady of a noble family, and was himself created a chief. Having had a quarrel with one of the natives, he resolved to pray him to death. So he built a hut on the top of a hill, and periodically went up to his lofty retreat to pray John Young to death. His friends told him that his end would soon come, for his enemy was praying him to death. The brawny tar had been travelling too long over the world, and had weathered too many storms, to be alarmed by such a tale; so he collected several of his friends, and sallied up the hill. They soon built a hut alongside that of the man who was praying for his death, and both he and his friends united in one voice a counter-supplication, which so terrified the unfortunate native, that he went home discomfited. He felt that it was all over with him, and that he had been outprayed; becoming melancholy, he subsequently died. After this failure the natives became thoroughly convinced that it was quite impossible to pray a white man to death.

In the rainy season, when all is verdure, the scenery is exceedingly picturesque and beautiful. There is a road leading from the town through the valley of Nuanu, where there are many neat and commodious villas belonging to the merchants. At the extremity of the valley is a deep precipice called Pali,* down which it is said Kamehameha the First, on his invasion of the island, drove the natives headlong in a terrible battle. The direct road to the opposite side of the island is by a winding pass, cut out of the face of this precipice. The island is divided by a range of mountains, stretching east and west; and on each side of the Pali they rise to a great height, looking like the huge lofty portals of this narrow gorge, through which the north-east trade-wind rushes violently, and sometimes with great fury, encountering the traveller as he commences to descend the opposite side. Here a noble prospect of the plain or district of Palikoolau amply repays the visitor for his ride. To the right and left the range of mountains which forms

---

* In the Hawaiian language "pali" means "precipice."

the backbone of the island, rise majestically and nobly. Towards the south they slope gently towards Honolulu and the sea; but on the north side they rise from the plains below like a perpendicular wall, varying from two to three thousand feet and upwards in height. Against this huge gigantic barrier the north-east trade-wind hurls dark and solemn clouds big with rain, which break against the rocky towers, cutting deep fissures in its haggard face like wrinkles wrought by the rude hand of Time.

At a few miles distant to the east and west, spurs of smaller hills extend outwards from the main range towards the north, forming a mighty and extensive amphitheatre, encircling a valley, beautiful in its rich tropical luxuriance. This group of islands are of volcanic origin; in some there are volcanoes now in operation, but in Oahu they are entirely extinct. If, upon further investigation, it could be proved that this valley had ever been the crater of a volcano, with one side now burst out by some great convulsion of nature, we may be able to form some idea of the magnitude of this monarch of fires in the days of its activity.

To all this natural beauty one historical incident invests the Pali with a kind of respect and awe in the estimation of the native. To the Kanaka his sea-girt home is his kingdom; it is his little world; he has his ancestors, and his stories to tell about them as well as ourselves; he can tell of the conquest of Oahu, when the forces of Kalani Kupule and Kaiana were routed by the victorious troops of Kamehameha the First, and how many of them, after being driven up the valley of Nuanu, were precipitated headlong down the Pali and destroyed.

But from the Pali another scene of peculiar interest is presented to the view. It is when the eye is turned from contemplating the works of God in all their sublimity and grandeur, to the little missionary station of Kaneohe, about four miles from the foot of the pass, where you may see a self-denying missionary and his family making humble efforts to bring back the wandering and reclaim the lost. There you may see the house of prayer, the school-house, and missionary's residence, where exertions are made not merely to reclaim the waste lands of the smiling valley, but, what is of infinitely greater importance, to reclaim the lost and ruined sons and daughters of Adam, whose souls present a waste, a moral wilderness, more appalling and more deserving of our utmost solicitude than the wastes and wilds of nature. For ages Satan reigned supreme with undisputed sway over the ruins of this section of the human race; but now men's hearts are moved towards the heathen, and feel themselves bound to obey the orders of our Divine Master in proclaiming peace to them who are afar off as well as to them who are nigh. There is also a Roman Catholic missionary settlement here, as well as a school for the better class, which is also under their control. These missionaries were forced upon the islanders by the French, who sent ships of war there for the purpose of reducing them into compliance. They do not seem to be well received either by the government or the mass of the people; but when restless spirits get tired of the religion in which they have been educated, or take offence at the minister who may be placed over them, they change sides and attend the Roman Catholic chapel, which is intended as a punishment to their former pastor, and thus a considerable congregation is collected.

14th May.—Set sail from Honolulu, and passing by the Philippine Islands, cast anchor on the 19th of June at Hongkong. When war was proclaimed with China, some of the vessels on the Pacific station were ordered across to take part in this expedition. The "Pearl" was one of the ships selected for this service, and it was for this reason that she was directed to make a voyage so unusual and so distant from the station to which she was originally sent. Troops were on their voyage out from England, and extensive preparations were making to strike an effective blow in reducing the Emperor of the Celestial Kingdom to terms, and convince him of the necessity of opening his ports to the commerce of the world. But no opportunity was afforded to the "Pearl" to take a very large or active share in these operations. More important military achievements were to be accomplished, and more valuable service was to be done. During the month the "Pearl" was in China, her men were only once in action against the enemy, when they were sent on a boat expedition to destroy some Chinese pirates. The method adopted to distinguish between a pirate and an honest trader is not very consonant to our ideas of discerning character. When a Chinese guide was once asked by the commanding officer whether the vessels seen a-head were the pirates, he recommended, as a test, that a few shots should be fired among them, remarking that honest men would not run away, but remain quietly in their ships; but that if they were pirates, they would "makey woilo," that is, they would desert their ships and make their escape. This would be rather an unsatisfactory test to the innocent ones, if any such there be; doubts are afloat on this point, however, arising from the fact that numbers of the Chinese vessels are armed, and it is strongly suspected that if they do not succeed in carrying on a little trade legitimately, they do not scruple to try the other way. They do not object to make money honestly if they can, but at any rate they like to make money.

It was when we were lying at anchor at Hongkong that the intelligence of the atrocities committed in India reached us. At first it was scarcely understood: it was not known whether it was a partial outbreak or a national revolt; but matters appeared to wear a more gloomy aspect when the report spread abroad that the Governor-General of India had despatched a most urgent requisition to Lord Elgin to send the troops to India which were daily expected out for the Chinese war. The truth then seemed to show out in all its alarming extent.

On the 15th July orders were issued to H.M.S. ships "Shannon" and "Pearl" to prepare for sea, and next day both ships weighed anchor and sailed for Calcutta. Lord Elgin was on board the "Shannon;" and three hundred of the R. M. L. Infantry having lately arrived in H.M.S. "Sanspareil," were immediately sent in the same vessel to Calcutta.

On arriving at Singapore, we found that H.M. 90th Regiment, which had a short time previously been wrecked in the "Transit," was awaiting a passage to India. Two companies were sent on board, and the ship being got ready for sea, we steamed through the straits, and made the best of our way to the mouth of the Hoogly. On arriving at the sand heads on the 7th of August, no pilot was to be procured; they were taking their ease in Calcutta, while for three days we were beating about in search of one, tost by a tempestuous south-west monsoon, at a time that the country was in a state of revolt and troops urgently required; and while their detention might have been most disastrous, the crisis in the capital of India being at its height.

After capturing one of these valuable functionaries, we proceeded up the Hoogly to Calcutta, and made fast to moorings off the Esplanade. The two companies of the 90th Regiment disembarked on the 12th of August, and were immediately sent up country.

CHAPTER III.

Royal Marines garrison Fort William—The Mohurrum at Calcutta—Naval Brigade embarked in the "Chunar"—Quarters in Buxar—Naval Brigade at Chupra—Camp at Myrwa—The Attack on Goothnee—The Rebels advance to Sohunpore—The first Alarm.

AT the time of our arrival one panic at Calcutta had just died away, and another was coming to a head. The Mohurrum, which is the great Mahomedan festival, was about to commence, and fears were excited that Mussulman fanaticism, which is generally brimful, would now boil over. Reports were spread of arms concealed, of rebels ready to rise, and Sepais ripe for massacre. Calcutta was put into an attitude of defence, some of the large public buildings were garrisoned by the volunteers who enrolled themselves in the ranks for mutual protection. The Royal Marines which came from China were quartered in Fort William, and orders were issued that the crew of the "Pearl" should be in readiness, the men being frequently landed for drill and the exercise of light field-guns. At last the Mohurrum passed away, and the alarm along with it— the preparations were too much for any Bengalee rebellion. The authorities were becoming wide-awake to the magnitude of the exigency; and, if the truth was known, it is highly probable that the natives were as much alarmed at the military arrangements that were made, as the Europeans were at their deficiency compared with the extent of the apprehended danger. At any rate, the Mohurrum went off more quietly than usual; whether it was that the Mussulmans were disappointed at their hopes being defeated, and their designs being frustrated, or fear lest the smallest disturbance would give occasion for an attack by European troops, from whom they had no reason to expect mercy, deponent saith not. The fears, however, of the European population who had taken refuge on board the ships on the river a few weeks before, became allayed; and the knowledge that the destructive broadsides of two ships of war could have been brought to bear on the city, burning the native population out of house and home, no doubt contributed to hush the murmurs of rebellion into silence, and render general the sense of security.

But the aspect of affairs was still gloomy: —a cloud hung over India; Delhi had not fallen; Lucknow was in the hands of the rebels; and shortly after a Chuckledar waved his standard over the rich and fertile province of Goruckpore.

Captain Peel, R.N. had volunteered, on his arrival, to bring the crew of H.M.S. " Shannon" and his heavy guns to the walls of Delhi. His offer was gladly accepted, and he left Calcutta about a week after his arrival. This design, however, was not carried out, but subsequently his guns were brought into position before the city of Lucknow. Captain Sotheby, R.N., also volunteered his services to the government, which were accepted; and on the 12th of September, 1857, he embarked a part of the crew of H.M.S. "Pearl," on board a small paddle-wheel steamer, called the "Chunar." The first detachment of the Naval Brigade to be followed by another company a month subsequently, consisted of 158 men of the "Pearl," including seamen and marines; one 12-pounder howitzer, one 24-pounder howitzer, and 24-pounder rockets.

The "Chunar," I believe, was one of the best steamers that could be obtained at the time; but bad was the best. If the stream was running strong, she was warranted "not to go;" in fact, a more deplorable conveyance for sending troops expeditiously up country could scarcely be found. The absence of railways was now experienced to be a want that no other means could so adequately supply, when a quick transport of troops would have been of such advantage to the State.

There is little of interest in the river scenery. Rank tropical luxuriance everywhere prevails; the banks of the river are low, and for some miles from Calcutta you may see large houses belonging to European merchants or native baboos. The burning Ghats near Calcutta are a novel sight. Here the bodies of the deceased Hindoos are committed to the flames: the smouldering corpse is deserted by those held dear in life, and the last offices of the dead are left to be performed by strangers who are regarded as the lowest caste, and despised for their profession and their pains. No friends remain to see the last offices performed with decency or order; but dogs, vultures, and adjutants frequent the spot to pick up the fragments that remain.

Sometimes the ghastly corpse of a Hindoo whose friends are too poor to buy fuel for the burning-pile, floats down the river, on which a vulture or carrion crow sails along to obtain his wonted repast. Such customs, like many others, are repulsive to Christian ideas of decency and propriety, and, like a multitude of other Eastern usages are the reverse of our own.

Occasionally a herd of cattle may be seen swimming across the river to the opposite bank, guided by the herdsmen, who cling to their backs with all the tenacity of monkeys. Their numerous heads just appearing above water, present an odd sight; more particularly so when a passing steamer suddenly blows off steam with a loud noise. Then there is a precipitate hurry-scurry and helter-skelter. They make as much haste as possible to escape. We need not, however, be surprised at the alarm of the dumb animal, when even their sable masters exhibit a similar fear. It is not uncommon to see them, while gazing from the banks on the "fire ship," take fright, and scatter in all directions, at the sudden blast from the blow-pipe. Bengalees are an exceedingly timid race. I have seen villagers run from the banks when a spy-glass was presented to the eye, supposing it to be a gun, and some who stood courageous for a few minutes, when a spy-glass was presented a second time, thought discretion the better part of valour.

16th September.—Passed the site of the battle-field of Plassey, which decided the fate of India one hundred years ago. For many years a well-known tree was flourishing here called Clive's tree; but the river has no respect for trees or fields, so it has washed away the one, and flows over the other. On the 17th, anchored off Burhampore. Near this place is Moorshedabad, where the Government has built a noble palace for the Nabob; in which, however, he is not supposed to reside. It contains a fine suite of apartments for show, but his private residence is adjacent, where he spends the greater part of his time. When coals were shipped, we proceeded steaming next day up the Bhaugaretti, and on the 21st entered the Ganges, that mighty artery of India. We had not gone far up the river when the pilot lodged complaints against a Brahmin called Chummun Sing regarding his threats to maltreat or murder the river pilots if they continued to bring steamers up the river for Europeans, telling the people that the Company's raj was at end. To permit this Brahmin to spread these reports, and use these threats with impunity, would have been productive of much inconvenience to the public service in terrifying the pilots from their duty or rendering them disaffected; it was therefore deemed advisable to bring the offender at once to punishment. On arriving at the village where he resided, a messenger was sent by Captain Sotheby, who was in command of the Naval Brigade, to summon the head policeman of the village, who requested to be excused on the grounds of being sick. Another policeman was procured, who rather reluctantly accompanied a party of marines to apprehend Chummun Sing. On being found, the policeman played false by denying him; but being unmistakeably identified, he was brought on board the "Chunar," and the case was investigated. The policeman was reported to the magistrate of the district, for attempting to shield the prisoner from punishment, and the prisoner was sent to the same magistrate to be dealt with according to his offence. During the rainy season the land in many parts of Bengal is covered with water, and presents the appearance of a dismal swamp, while the huts of the inhabitants looked wretched and comfortless in the middle of a land inundated with waters. It is the former, however, which renders the country a fertile garden; and the latter, though so miserable, seem to satisfy the wants of a simple people, who are averse to change, even for the better, the construction of their hovels. There is very little in the scenery to relieve the monotony of a dull cruise up the Ganges: it was not sufficient to know that the barren and desolate-looking banks from which the waters were fast receding, would, in a short time, be covered with crops and vegetation, the eye wanted something attractive to rest on as well as the imagination. From Moorshedabad to Dinapore, which was reached on the 7th of October, there was no station of any importance except Rajmahal, Bhaugulpore, and Monghyr. The first was once a royal residence, as its name imports; and there are still to be seen the fine old ruins of a palace, with some curious arches and tracery-work remaining; but the greater part of the building has fallen to decay, or has been precipitated into the river by the stream, which has not ceased for years to undermine its foundations. The second is a civil station, with the usual staff of civilians for the management of the district. Here missionary operations are carrie on with considerable vigour and success. The Santals and Hill men, among whom the missionary labours, have fewer prejudices to break down, and present fewer obstacles to the embracing of Christianity than the Hindoo, and therefore afford a favourable field for labour. Monghyr is also a civil station, and one of the most picturesque on the river. It is an old square fortress, surrounded by high walls with a ditch outside, enclosing within a considerable space, sufficient for many fine houses and gardens. It is also defended by small towers and bastions; but not having been repaired for years past, they are falling to decay. Within these spacious grounds there is a church, as well as one at Bhaugulpore; but neither having a Government chaplain, they are dependent on the voluntary services of missionaries for ministerial duty. Monghyr also lays claim to the name of a manufacturing town, and has been denominated the Birmingham of India; though by what right its friends assume for it that title I am at a loss to discover. The natives here possess the faculty of manufacturing chairs, tables, and other furniture; they can carve ornaments in wood and horn, such as bracelets, chains, and ornamental walking-sticks; they also manufacture fire-arms and other iron work; but their ingenuity does not seem to be of a very high cast, or to take a very wide range.

On the 7th of August, on arriving at Dinapore, the 24-pound howitzer was left behind to be sent back to the ship; since no gun-carriage fit for land-service could be procured for it, either from the arsenal or at Dinapore. One 12-p^r howitzer and two 12-p^r mountain train-guns were supplied in its place.

Captain Sotheby received orders that the Naval Brigade under his command should proceed to Buxar and garrison the fort there. Having reached it on the 10th, the guns, ammunition and baggage being landed, they took up their quarters in the fort which had been prepared for their reception. Buxar was once a civil station, and is soon to be so again, but its importance at that time chiefly consisted in one of the principal government studs for breeding cavalry horses being in the neighbourhood. And in consequence of the mutiny of so many cavalry regiments, it was of considerable importance to keep a good look-out for those that remained in order to supply the place of those that had been taken off by the mutineers. During the time that the Naval Brigade was quartered in the fort at Buxar no time was lost; the men were drilled daily, and were exercised at gunnery with unremitting care. In a short time, they were proficients in the exercise of the field-guns and the management of the artillery horses; in fact, they were rapidly becoming soldiers.

On the 23rd of October orders were received directing the Naval Brigade to proceed immediately to Chupra, an alarm having arisen from a report that a body of rebels were hovering on the borders of the district of Sarun. This district was rich and fertile, the treasury was full and tempting, and therefore precautionary measures were urgently required to prevent it meeting with the same fate as some others. That evening a detachment, under the command of Lieutenant Grant, R.N., was sent over in a small river-steamer, the distance being about five-and-thirty or forty miles. And on the 26th the remainder, with the guns, ammunition, and baggage, followed, landing at Chupra Ghat in the afternoon of the same day. The school-house was fitted up to receive them, but these quarters were not long enjoyed. As soon as hackeries and baggage-carts could be procured, they marched to Sewan, a small town forty miles to the north of Chupra. This town had, some time previously, been abandoned by the European residents on the occasion of the incursion of the rebels in that quarter; but was at this time reoccupied by a regiment of Gorkhas, having lately arrived, and giving some degree of security and confidence to the peaceable portion of the inhabitants.

The rebel forces began collecting in

formidable numbers on the borders of the district; and threatening a friendly Rajah at Mujowlee, not more than six-and-twenty miles distant, it was deemed advisable to take up a more advanced position; and consequently, by the orders of Captain Sotheby, R.N., the force, consisting of the Naval Brigade and a regiment of Gorkhas, made one march to Myrwa in advance. This movement had the effect of diverting the rebels from attacking Mujowlee for that time. Prospects of a most serious character seemed to threaten the valuable districts of Sarun, Chumparun, and Tirhoot. The Sepais at this time managing to inspire the public with a very exalted idea of their courage and dangerous ferocity, serious apprehensions of consequences of the most calamitous nature were entertained by men in authority, if the rebels should succeed in making a sweeping invasion of the districts north of the Ganges with artillery, while there were no available troops to augment the Sarun field force, and enable it to make a determined resistance. It was felt that even Patna, to the south of the Ganges, was not safe: peril of no ordinary character would have hung over it if the districts on the other side of the river had fallen into the hands of the insurgents. The paucity of the European troops at this period of the war was felt in every direction. The only Europeans that could be spared to defend these extensive provinces was the Naval Brigade, which had lately been augmented by another company under Lieutenant Radcliffe, R.N., numbering altogether about two hundred and fifty officers and men. Some of them had been raised by volunteers among the merchant seamen at a time when every European was of such great value; but the great majority were men-of-war seamen belonging to H.M. steam ship "Pearl" and her detachment of Royal Marines.

It may seem a misapplication of a name to apply the term "Brigade" to so small a number as two hundred and fifty men; but the Naval Brigade in the Crimea having consisted of a very strong force, to it the term may with propriety have been applied; and no definite name being generally given to a body of seamen when landed for service on shore, they seem to have inherited that title from the distinguished band who served on shore during the Russian war; and hence it seems to have been adopted, without reference to numbers, by seamen engaged in lånd service. It was not unusual to read in some of the Indian newspapers, during the time of the mutinies, about the movements of some Naval Brigade consisting of a hundred merchant-seamen serving in different parts of India; consequently, if this is admissible, it need not be considered out of place to denominate a body of seamen and Royal Marines of H.M.

navy by the same name. The difference between service on shore and afloat now presented commissariat and other difficulties, which in an incredible short space of time were overcome. Lieutenant Grant, R.N., who had previously been given charge of the treasure-chest, was also appointed staff officer, and in addition acted as paymaster and commissariat officer—offices which he continued to fulfil for several months, until it became necessary (the brigade being augmented by other European troops) to have a commissariat officer, Lieutenant Bolton, attached to the force. On the 27th of November Colonel Rowcroft, who had commanded the 8th Regiment of Native Infantry which mutinied at Dinapore, arrived at Myrwa to take command of the Sarun Field Force. Operations were to be carried on entirely on the defensive, and at this time, on no account was Goruckpore to be entered, as the force was not sufficiently strong to attack the enemy with effect, and other troops could not be spared.

For several weeks the force was encamped at Myrwa, and no enemy showed himself; occasionally a Brahmin, a spy or budmash, would be captured and executed; but there was no advancing army reported. The men began to despair of seeing the mutineers; they began to think that they were brought up country for nothing, and thought it very hard to be left in the background where there was no opponent, while others were pressing to the front. Disappointment became general that they could not have a "crack" at the Sepais. This state of repose was not destined to last long. On the 13th of December a report was brought in that the rebels had attacked Goothnee, a village about eight miles distant, had plundered the magazine, and had driven out the small garrison of Sikhs which were left to defend the town. Colonel Rowcroft ordered a detachment of the Naval Brigade, with four guns, a detachment of the Ramdhul regiment of Gorkhas, and a detachment of the Royal Marines, to march without delay to Goothnee, and drive them out. On arriving at the place about noon, a true account of the affair became known. The alarm was occasioned by a small force of the rebels having crossed the river during the night, the Sikhs were taken by surprise, being utterly unprepared for an attack: and their Jemandar in command, being an old Brahmin, maintained no discipline, and allowed them to live in a disorderly manner; and who, when the Sikhs were assembled, would not lead them out against the insurgents. The Jemandar was made prisoner and sent to Dinapore for trial.* The Sikhs were ashamed of having left their post, volunteered any service to retrieve their

---

* He was afterwards transported.

character, and threw the blame on the Jemandar. On the other side of the river which flows past Goothnee, the rebels were numerous, but it was not considered prudent to attack them with so small a force, and in the evening the men returned to Myrwa.

On the 18th our camping ground was changed to a more desirable position on the left bank of the river Jurrai, and strong piquets were posted in front and on both flanks. This movement was necessary, arising from the fact that the information was not always reliable, and the number of the insurgents might turn out to be (as subsequently was discovered) much greater than at first reported; it was, therefore, deemed desirable to have the river as a defence in front, instead of being a barrier immediately in rear of our camp, in the event of the enemy coming down with very superior numbers. The rebels being usually shortsighted, and not probably understanding the cause of this apparent retreat, were emboldened by it to advance; and encouraging their followers with the notion that we were weak and retreating, crossed the little Gunduck at Mujowlee on the 22nd, and a day or two afterwards took up a position about seven miles in our front, in topes (of trees) near the village of Sohunpore, where they threw up earthworks in front of their camp. This apparent retreat, which was only intended as a precautionary movement, had the effect of drawing them on to an engagement in the open field; an opportunity which, in all probability, would not otherwise have been so freely given.

The Sarun Field Force only consisted, at this time, of 250 of the Naval Brigade, with four guns, including a detachment of forty-five of the Royal Marine Light Infantry, and about 450 of the Ramdhul regiment of Gorkhas, fifty of them having been left at Sewan with a small detachment of seamen.

On the 24th, the day before Christmas, the alarm was given of the approach of the enemy, which numbered several thousands. The troops were soon under arms, and the artillery horses were got ready for the guns. After waiting an hour without any prospect of an enemy, the spies who were sent out for intelligence, brought back word that quietness in every direction prevailed, and no rebels were to be seen beyond their piquets, a few sowars who were observed on the road on a reconnoitring excursion causing the alarm.

All prospect of seeing the rebels that day was banished, and the men went to their tents disappointed. Next day being Christmas, and having no prospect of a plum-pudding, Jack jocularly expressed his disappointment at not having a " sea-pie" (Sepoy).

CHAPTER IV.

Arrival of a Gorkha Regiment—Gorkha Arms—Action at Sohunpore—Flight of the Enemy—Their Camp taken—Sarun saved—Activity of Seamen in the management of Horses—All difficulties overcome—Defenceless state of the Country—Advantages of this Victory — Advance on Roodurpore—Punishment of Rebels.

DECEMBER 25th.—This morning the Field Force received a reinforcement of the Gorucknath regiment of Gorkhas, 500 strong. It was now our turn to produce a little alarm among the enemy; but having come by forced marches from Segowlee, they were too much fatigued, footsore, and hungry to march again that day; and consequently the Christmas-day was passed in peace and quietness. Notwithstanding this augmentation to our force, the prospect was not particularly promising. The insurgents numbered several thousands, the Gorkhas were still untried, and they were armed with the old flint-lock muskets, which were by no means equal to the Brown Bess of the Sepais; nevertheless, it was resolved to attack and beat them the following day. The Nepalese did not rejoice in a strikingly Hyde-Park appearance; but they turned out occasionally to have plenty of "pluck" when led by Europeans. Each regiment numbers about 500. The Ramdhul had red coats, and the Gorucknath blue: the cut is not very describable; it was evidently intended to be after the fashion of the coatee. There was a scarf over their shoulders, rather brownish, but intended for white; and trousers of a similar colour, the cut of which was something between French and Turkish. The religion of the men in the former regiment was Hindoo, regarding the ox as a sacred animal; and consequently orders were issued by Government that no bullocks should be killed in the vicinity of their camp, that their prejudices should not be violated. The other was raised in that part of Nepal bordering on Tibet, and would eat the flesh of the buffalo without any conscientious scruples.

Christmas-day passed in peace. Towards evening rumours were afloat that the rebels were to be attacked next morning. Orders were issued a little later in the evening by Colonel Rowcroft that put it beyond all doubt, and all went to rest awaiting the results of the morrow.

December 26th.—Having breakfasted earlier than usual, the force under the command of Colonel Rowcroft left the camp about eight o'clock, A.M., to meet the enemy. One hundred Gorkhas, fifty matchlock men of the Hutwah Rajah, and a few seamen were left to protect the camp and guard the bridge across the Jurrai, which was on the high road leading from Myrwa to Sohunpore.

The force which got ready to march was the Naval Brigade, 180 men and four guns, 12-p^r howitzers under the command of Captain Sotheby, R.N., including thirty of the Royal Marine Light Infantry under Lieutenant Pym, fifty Sikhs under the command of Lieutenant Burlton, 500 of the Ramdhul regiment of Gorkhas, and 350 of the Gorucknath regiment, under the command of Captains Weston and Brooks. The Hon. Victor Montague, midshipman, was appointed acting aide-de-camp to Colonel Rowcroft, and Mr. F. H. Stephenson, midshipman, was acting aide-de-camp to Captain Sotheby, R.N. This duty they continued to fulfil throughout both campaigns. Mr. Foot, midshipman, was attached to Lieutenant Turnour's light field battery; and Lieutenant Radcliffe was in command of the naval column.

The line of march having been previously arranged, the force kept along the road leading from Myrwa (where the camp was left standing) to Sohunpore, about seven miles distant. Along the line of march the column was in sections, preceded by the Sikhs in skirmishing order; and the Marines, under Lieutenant Pym, followed as a reserve to the Sikhs, in case of an attack.

It had been ascertained that the rebels were posted in two or three large topes (groves of mango-trees) near the village of Sohunpore, on both sides of the road leading to Mujhowlee, and that three of their four guns, with a numerous body as a support, were posted behind a high bank, with the additional cover afforded by a large tank. Having arrived within a mile of this position, the force deployed into line, taking ground to the right. Lieutenant Pym, with a detachment of the Royal Marines, and Lieutenant Grant, R.N., with a detachment of seamen, advanced skirmishing on the right Lieutenant Burlton, with the Sikh skirmishers, were on the left. The four 12-p^r howitzers were in the centre; at some distance to the right of the guns, the naval column deployed into line; a detachment of the Gorucknath regiment were between the Marines and the naval column; and the Ramdhul regiment formed line on the left of the guns; a reserve of two companies of Gorkhas were in rear of the line, and the spare artillery bullocks, spare ammunition carts and elephants, were drawn up in rear of the reserve with a rear-guard. As it was the intention to follow them up as closely as it was possible with infantry, and hold all the ground that might be gained, two days' provisions and two or three tents were brought with the force, no other baggage being allowed to leave the camp. The first gun was fired about ten o'clock, A.M., and disclosed the enemy's position. Sowars, or Native Cavalry, were seen hovering on the left, while on the right

and in front were large bodies of infantry.
Our force deployed into line in a large open
maidan or plain; but intervening between
our men and the enemy were fields of high
crops, such as sugar-cane, dhal, and other
grain, and which grew so high that a large
army might lie concealed in it, while the
country would present the appearance of the
most placid repose. The enemy pushed
forward numerous skirmishers into the topes
(woods) and high crops, opening a heavy
fire of guns and musketry. Our skirmishers, though few, also advanced, steadily and
boldly, driving them back, and doing much
execution with their rifles. Notwithstanding
the thick cover by which they might have
been concealed, the noise and tumult which
prevails in a native camp soon discovered
the position of their main body. Their left
was resting on the village of Sohunpore, and
their right on a small village in which they
had planted two guns. As soon as our line

had advanced within range, it was received by a heavy fire from the guns which were in position in the village on the left. These guns enfiladed our line, which then fell back and changed front. The Naval Artillery in reply fired several rounds of shot and shell in rapid succession. The line advanced, and approached close to the village, from which a fire of musketry was still kept up. Other guns opened fire on our line from our front, and a brisk cannonade was kept up on all sides. The firing of the Naval Artillery, under Lieutenant Turnour, R.N., was kept up with great precision and telling effect, silencing two of the enemy's guns, which were posted on our left, in half an hour. Once the Sowars made a movement as if with the intention to charge; but the incessant fire of the artillery produced a change in their movements, and checked their advance. A few well-directed shell, pitching in the midst, scattered them in all directions.

A large body of infantry then moved towards a village on our left, apparently with a view to outflank us; but the Sikhs, supported by two companies of Gorkhas, advanced, and took the village, which they held throughout the day; while the Royal Marines under Lieutenant Pym, and a party of seamen under Lieutenant Grant, R.N., entered Sohunpore on the right. Their movements then becoming completely paralysed, they retired in great confusion. After a three-hours' hard fight, the enemy was completely dispersed and driven off the field. They were expelled from the topes and village, which was then entered. Their camp was taken and burned, some tents were carried off by the Sikhs, while their dinner and other articles, including earthenware culinary utensils, were left on the ground.

Their number was estimated at 6000; of which 1200 were regular Sepais, and 150 were cavalry. Their loss was supposed to be about 150, and their principal leaders were Hurkishen Sing and the Naib Nazim Mushuruff Khan. A few of them held the village for some time after the main body had fled, to cover their retreat, as on entering, it was discovered that they had gone for some time with their guns, flying precipitately by Mujhowlee towards Goruckpore.

Throughout the action they never ventured nearer to our line than four or five hundred yards, the shell and rifles keeping them at this respectful distance; and as our line steadily and firmly advanced, they judiciously, but precipitately, retired. The Gorkhas, under the direction of Captains Weston and Brooks, behaved steadily and stood firmly throughout the day ; but their arms, being the old flint-musket, did little execution, and therefore to the shell and rifle success was universally acknowledged to be due.

Disorganized and routed, they were followed up in hot pursuit. If cavalry had formed a part of our force, their defeat would have been rendered still more disastrous. On approaching Mujhowlee, the rear of the rebel forces came in sight. The Marines, a part of the Naval Brigade, and four companies of the Gorucknath regiment were ordered to push rapidly on after the Sikhs, who composed the advanced guard, in hopes of capturing the guns, as they were fording the river. They were soon pounced upon by the Sikhs; one large iron gun was taken with limber complete, full of ammunition, and several of the enemy were killed. Two tumbrils, one full of ammunition, and the other of powder, were also taken.

But one circumstance above all others which is a matter of wonder as well as thankfulness, is, that, while inflicting so severe a blow on the enemy, so little loss should be sustained by ourselves. There was only one killed, and he was a camp follower; several, however, were wounded, although only one or two, who were Gorkhas, severely. Fortunately the gun and musket-firing of the rebels is generally too high, the balls passing over the heads of the troops in the line, tearing up the ground, and ricocheting harmlessly in the rear.

The day by this time was drawing to a close, and the men had had a hard day's work of ten hours, and a fourteen-miles march under an Indian sun, when they returned to the village of Mujhowlee, and bivouacked for the night. They were fagged, and tired with running, and required rest. The excitement for a time took away the thoughts of heat and hunger; but a bit of bread and a glass of grog was not to be refused. The Rajah came out to meet the troops and give a hearty welcome, as also did the villagers along the road, who supplied water to quench the parching thirst of the men while marching in thick clouds of dust and under a burning sun. Their salaams were most humble, and apparently as sincere as most Hindoo compliments. They were, at any rate, glad to make friends with the winning side, and no doubt felt the difference between the conduct of our troops and that of their own countrymen, who for several days had been looting all the villages in the vicinity of their camp. On the other hand, a locomotive bazaar or market having been established, marched when our force marched, and the natives, finding the trade so lucrative, were glad to bring their goods, knowing that they would obtain a ready sale and a good price.

The Rajah of Mujhowlee had suffered severely by the looting and plundering of his villages; and they coolly told him that, upon becoming masters of the country, they would divest him of a portion of his landed property, but that a portion of it he should be permitted to retain. The Rajah also stated that the insurgents advanced with the full persuasion of being able to surround and destroy so small a force, and then to overrun Sarun, Chunparun, and Tirhoot, raising the districts in rebellion.

There are few actions on record, if any, in which so small a number of European troops encountered and completely defeated an enemy so numerous; and seldom has one day's work been known so completely to clear a district of a horde of marauding rebels, rescuing many villages from plunder and oppression.

Asiatics can by no means be compared to European troops, and never can be so depended on; and although the Nepalese may be active in climbing the crags of their native hills, and be formidable when defending the fastnesses and homes in their native jungles, yet that an enemy numbering 6000, or perhaps more, should be dispersed and scattered when 200 European troops were engaged, aided by these Nepalese, is an evidence of what the boldness and daring of British troops will do. And when it is remembered that they were British seamen and marines, the former of whom were entirely out of their element—who, from being sailors by profession, were marshalled as soldiers—who, from riding over the boisterous billows of the foaming deep, were drilled to ride the horses of the Naval Artillery, and while they pursued the enemy with a rapidity and perseverance not to be outstripped, the 12-pounder howitzers discharged shot and shell on their retreating and broken ranks with a precision and effect not to be surpassed, eliciting the praise from the commanding officer that the "troops behaved as British seamen and marines ever do, most excellently and gallantly. Captain Sotheby, being everywhere present with the guns in action, having paid great attention to the drill and training of the men for land service," for which "they are now ready, horses having been trained for the guns, and seamen to ride them and act as gunners."

And thus, under the influence of good discipline, artillery practice and drill, the men invariably gained the approbation of those by whom they were commanded, for valour in the field as well as good conduct in the camp.

During the halts at Sewan and Myrwa the Brigade was exercised daily at battalion and light-infantry drill, rifle-practice, and light field-piece drill. The horses at first were fresh and unbroken, and when yoked to the guns, carried away the traces; but in a short time they were so well managed, that when they came into action, they had advanced to a high degree of efficiency, not only in those duties in which the requirements of their profession as men-of-war's men caused them

to be acquainted, such as rifle-practice and
gunnery, but to their wonted activity in the
management of guns was added a speedily
acquired expertness in the management of
the artillery horses. But the difficulty of
raising this corps to such a high state of
efficiency was more than ordinary, arising
from the impossibility of procuring the necessary stores from the arsenals. Guns were
supplied; but spare ammunition-wagons,
limbers, and horses were deficient, and when
with great difficulty and perseverance horses
were procured, it was found necessary to get
the greater part of the harness made in camp,
not being able to get sufficient saddlery
supplied; and, instead of having spare ammunition-wagons and limbers drawn by
horses, which is necessary to the efficiency
of a battery, the only substitute that could
be procured was hackeries, or native carts
drawn by bullocks, and warranted to go two
or two and a half miles an hour by a vigo-

rous application of the stick. A limber or spare ammunition-wagon was nowhere to be procured until after the first action, when those taken from the enemy, on that and other occasions, were, by the vigorous ingenuity and diligence of the ship's carpenter, Mr. Burton, converted to our own use, affording an example of that readiness with which a sailor can turn his hand to anything, and get out of a difficulty while many a man would be thinking about it.

Inconsiderable as this force may seem to have been, the results and moral effect of this victory were of great importance, when it is remembered that a few days prior to the engagement, some of the most valuable and productive districts in India, from which a large revenue is collected, were threatened by several thousand rebels, many of the zemindars being disaffected and likely to render assistance to the enemy, and, as has since been discovered, their plans and expectations had been to surround by their superior numbers and cut up the little force at Myrwa, and then march direct and unopposed into the district of Sarun, where there was not a European soldier from the banks of the Ganges to the frontier of Nepaul, except the Naval Brigade.* But the tide turned; the wave which seemed destined to sweep over the fertile plains dashed against a rock, from which it receded broken and abased. Confidence was restored in the district, disaffected zemindars paid their rents in silence, and thus, though the force employed was small, the advantages derived from the success were considerable. And when it is remembered that it was obtained without the loss of a single man, a few only being wounded, ought we not to be led to

---

* About this time the Bengal Yeomanry Cavalry crossed the Ganges at Patna into the district of Tirhoot, in number 200.

believe that the High and Mighty One who is the only Giver of all victory, showed a favour unto us, crowning our arms with success.

For several days successively, prisoners continued to be taken, one of whom was a Sepai of the 10th Regiment of Native Infantry. Following the routine at that period of the war, he was blown away from a gun in the presence of the assembled troops, explanations having been given to the Gorkhas that this was not the English method of treating prisoners taken in war, but was only inflicted in this special case when the crime committed was stained with peculiar heinousness. As was usual with these men under similar circumstances, he walked up to the gun apparently with perfect indifference, was lashed to it with his back to the muzzle, and met his end with remarkable apathy. He acknowledged having been engaged on the 26th, and he must have been zealous in the cause he had espoused, for he had gone out to the battle unarmed, waiting to take the place of some fallen comrade, whose arms he could appropriate.

The Rajah of Mujhowlee was well pleased with the departure of the rebels, and often came into camp like a feudal baron, attended by the chief men of his household and armed retainers. His palace, however, did not present a very baronial appearance; nor did it appear to afford what we should regard as plain English comfort.

On the 27th the tents and baggage came from Myrwa to Mujhowlee, where we remained encamped until the 30th, when the camp was struck and the force crossed the Chota Gunduck, and pitched the camp on the right bank of the river, near the village of Sulempore. During the halt here the time was occcupied not only in discovering and punishing those who had been active in their opposition to Government, but in getting the best intelligence that could be procured regarding the retreat and probable movements of the rebels at Goruckpore. Many of the peaceably-disposed inhabitants who came to pay their respects and make their salaams to the magistrate, complained bitterly of the plundering of the rebels in all directions; in fact, when poultry or mess stock was sought for along the line of march, the invariable reply was that the Budmashes had looted it all. But as many of them were rebelliously disposed when European troops turned their backs, they were not so much to be pitied; and it is to be hoped that, having tasted the "Raj" of their own people, they may for the future be better contented with that of the British.

After a succession of marches, the force arrived at Roodurpore on the 11th of January, from which the Rajah had fled, taking with him his treasure and moveable property; a great part of which was afterwards discovered and captured. The town was nearly deserted, and the houses locked up. It was a case of "like master like man." The ryots follow the steps of the ruler. If he is a rebel, the chances are they will be rebels too, although they have no very clear conception of the reason for being so. Here the force remained encamped until the 22nd. During the halt a sale of the Rajah's property and effects took place, and the magistrate was enabled to organize a police, and get that part of the country a little settled.

On the 22nd the camp was struck, and the force left Roodurpore and marched to Gowra, a small village which carries on a trade in the boiling and preparing of sugar. The camp was pitched in a tope of trees, and without any prospect of a move for a few days. Some of the principal residents of this village were said to have been killed at Sohunpore, and many others in the vicinity were known to have been disaffected. Next day a detachment was sent to Pyena, about five miles distant, to punish some of the principal offenders; and the day following the force made a short march to Rajpore Ghat, on the river Raptee. Having been deluged here by a heavy fall of rain, the river was not crossed until the 27th, when the baggage, guns, &c., crossed in boats, and the men followed in the afternoon. There was some trouble in crossing the baggage and guns in boats, but none in crossing the elephants. They take to the water as naturally as a spaniel, and swim. Their bodies disappear completely under water; the mahouts stand on their backs, while the huge proboscis appears over the surface, through which he breathes and occasionally utters most uncouth sounds. Along the river, as well as on the adjacent Jheels, there are abundance of wild duck, widgeon, a kind of snipe, and geese, affording plenty of occupation for sportsmen. The Ramdhul regiment of Gorkhas proceeded to Azimghur the same day as an escort for percussion-muskets (I believe 4000 stand of arms), which were to be brought back for the Nepalese troops with Jung Bahadoor, their own arms not being considered effective. The day following we marched to Burhul, on the left bank of the Gogra, which was on the high road from Goruckpore to Benares; and some importance being attached to the keeping of the Ghat, there was a halt here for several days, until, by the advance of the Nepalese troops, by whom Goruckpore had lately been taken, after a feeble resistance, and with whom the Sarun field force was to act in concert, the insurgents were known to be entirely driven far to the westward. There was reason to suppose that four regiments of cavalry and 4000 infantry were at Fyzabad, not more than five or six marches distant, and therefore there was an additional reason for keeping a good look-out on this part of the river, boats being required for the construction of a bridge across the Gogra for Jung Bahadoor's army, which was marching to Lucknow.

The time occupied by these numerous halts was not altogether thrown away, as an opportunity was given to the magistrate to make arrangements for the re-organization of the police, and the settlement of the district, while at the same time punishment was inflicted on the refractory zemindars by the destruction of their houses, and in such other ways as was most suitable. This, it must be acknowledged, does not seem to be a very chivalrous method of bringing the delinquent to terms, savouring something of the Goth; but to the native of India it is a most severe punishment, and peculiarly humiliating, being regarded as a great disgrace, and serves to keep up a wholesome dread in the minds of others, lest a similar fate should befal themselves. It is reported that at this part of the river, about Pyena and Burhuj, some of the most influential men impose a sort of duty or tax on boats passing up and down even in peaceable times, and therefore their punishment may be looked upon as an example of retributive justice for a double offence.

CHAPTER V.

The Fleet of Boats proceed up the Gogra—Captain Sotheby in Command of the Escort—Perilous Nature of the Expedition—Taking of the Fort of Chanderpore—The Crossing of the Gogra—Battle of Phoolpore—Gun turned upon the Enemy by the Royal Marines—A Kookrie Charge—Naval Brigade recross the Gogra—Prejudices of the Gorkhas regarding the Slaying of the Ox.

BY the 8th of February, 150 boats were procured, and a small steamer called the "Jumna" was in readiness to accompany them up the Gogra as far as Gai Ghat. Along her sides, bulwarks, and around her upper decks fascines were attached, to protect her as much as possible from shot, and the fire of musketry; presenting, in some degree, the appearance of a moving battery. The following day Mr. Fowler, an officer of the Naval Brigade, was sent on board the "Jumna" to take charge, and on the 10th the fleet of boats proceeded up the river as far as Ghopalpore, where the field force were encamped, having marched from Burhul the same day. The intelligence as to the state of the Oudh side of the river was not very favourable to such an undertaking. Various reports arrived as to the strength of the rebels in the different forts that overlooked the river, and from which a few rounds of shot and shell would not only destroy the boats, but even long before this would be effected, every native boatman would have fled in dismay and alarm, leaving the boats to their fate. It would, therefore, have been hazardous to allow the fleet to advance further up without a strong escort. It was ascertained with tolerable certainty that four or five thousand rebels were at Tandah; a town at no great distance from the place where the boats were required, from which a flying column might be detached by an enterprising and daring enemy (which fortunately experience showed was not their character), and being brought to bear on any one point, might sink the boats. Intelligence being defective, the whole of that part of the country on the Oudh side being entirely in the hands of the insurgents, the escort, if taken by surprise, might not only have suffered considerable loss, but have entered upon a fruitless enterprise, the enemy not only having the advantage of the eminence from the banks, but being able at any moment to choose their own point of attack, and retire at pleasure, until another favourable opportunity might be presented, when perhaps the boats, turning round a bend of the river, might be met by a galling fire from some thick jungle or from behind some wall or embankment.

After different plans were proposed and rejected, according to instructions received from Brigadier-General Macgregor, it was finally decided that the troops intended for the escort should be placed under the command of Captain Sotheby, R.N. They consisted of 145 seamen and marines, 100 Gorkhas, and 50 Sikhs, with one 12-pounder howitzer, in addition to the steamer "Jumna" with two small guns. It was supposed that sailors would then be in their element, and in the event of getting into a difficulty, would, no doubt, be well able to get out of it. The defective knowledge as to the strength of the forts on the river invested the expedition with some degree of peril; but it was of the utmost importance that it should be carried out with the least possible delay, that the bridging of the river might be completed in order to facilitate the transit of the Gorkhas to the siege of Lucknow.

About eight o'clock in the afternoon of the 13th of February, the troops for the escort duty left Seekregunge for Raibundpore Ghat, the place of embarkation, where they arrived about eleven o'clock at night, after a wearisome march across a country without roads. Here they pitched two small tents, their rations of rum were served out, and no persuasion was required to retire to rest. On the 16th, the head-quarters, under Colonel Rowcroft, marched to a place called Chupra Ghat, on the Gogra, where a brigade of Gorkhas had been sent by the orders of Jung Bahadoor to render any necessary assistance in the advance of the fleet; but being completely bound down by the orders of their chief, the European officers in military charge had little control over them, and were utterly unable to force them to yield their aid in the manner most required and most serviceable, rendering their assistance of little value. The following day one regiment of Gorkhas, with two guns, was persuaded to march in the direction of Chanderpore, a strong fort on the right bank of the Gogra, but, in obedience to Jung's orders, they refused to cross the river, except in company with the whole force, and the only advantage derived from their presence was, that they were present as spectators of the capture of the fort from the opposite bank.

After the escort reached Raibundpore Ghat, on the night of the 13th, it was detained there until next morning, when, after the embarkation in the steamer and some of the boats, there was considerable delay by means of a strong wind blowing down the river; but after ceaseless energy and perseverance, notwithstanding the obstacles of wind, current, the absence of a pilot, and clouds of sand, the boats constantly running foul of each other, and sometimes creating the utmost confusion, and notwithstanding the absence of both chart and pilot, the fleet advanced on the 17th as far as the strong fort of Chanderpore, on the right bank, at ten o'clock in the morning. Captain Sotheby landed about two miles below the fort, with 130 of the Naval Brigade, 35 Sikhs, and 60 Gorkhas. This fort, like many others in Oudh, which are now happily either destroyed or in the process of being destroyed, might, with a few brave defenders, have made a most successful resistance against a very superior force. It was constructed with a deep ditch and high embankment on all sides, except on that facing the river, where the height and precipitous nature of the embankments affording it sufficient strength, rendered a ditch unnecessary. Inside were rifle-pits and loopholed breastworks, approached by a zigzag path terminating with gates leading to a second set. It was also defended by strong bastions and a parapet, as well as substantial buildings in the centre, all loopholed. And, in addition to this, it was surrounded by a thick jungle of prickly bamboo, so close set as to be almost impenetrable. This latter defence, which, in the hands of brave soldiers, might be turned to good account, is used by these renowned warriors, the Rajpoots of Oudh, for the purpose of cover in making their escape. In their own intestine feuds it was* regarded a disgrace to run without making some appearance of a stand, and, therefore, they would resist the besiegers for a day or two with unconquerable bravery, in a place in which they were perfectly secure, until, according to their view of chivalry, they could retire from the strife, during the darkness of the night, under cover of the jungle, without any stain being cast on their gallantry, or slur on their military honour.

But on this occasion, having Europeans to contend with, they did not think it judicious to remain so long. After Captain

---

* This is written in the past tense, as it is hoped these feudal wars are past and gone for ever in India.

Sotheby had disembarked his men, the line being formed by the seamen, they advanced with a twelve-pounder mountain-train howitzer under Lieutenant Turnour, R.N. A body of marines and seamen skirmishers, with support of Sikhs under Captain Weston, 36th Regiment Native Infantry (the marines and seamen being in charge of Mr. Ingles, mate, R.N., and the Sikhs under Lieutenant Burlton), were pushed forward; and having passed through the village, which was found to be deserted, the skirmishers were received with a heavy fire of musketry and guns from the rebels concealed in the rifle-pits and fort. Captain Weston gallantly dashed forward, and was as gallantly followed; but in trying to force the gate, was severely wounded by a man inside, and immediately carried to the rear. The gun was then brought up within a hundred yards of the entrance, and under cover of a house, fired several rounds. At the same time Captain Sotheby sent orders to Mr. Fowler, R.N., to advance in the steamer "Jumna," and throw in a few rounds of grape and shot, which rattled through the bamboo; while at the same time the Gorkhas threatening their right, the defenders being afraid lest their retreat should be cut off, fled with all speed through the jungle in the rear, as the marines and Sikhs entered in the front.

There was much valuable property found in the fort, of which the Sikhs, as usually happens, laid hands on the lion's share. Two guns were taken, one six-pounder, and one four-pounder, with limbers, and one spare ammunition-wagon. The enemy were supposed to be about 300; their loss most probably was trifling, by reason of the thick cover under which they found shelter. The casualty list on our side was, two severely wounded, and two or three slightly, their firing being, as usual, too high—the bullets passed over the heads of our men. Having no cavalry, pursuit was impossible; and the object being attained, the adjacent buildings in the fort were burned, the piquets were withdrawn, and the men re-embarked.

Brigadier-General Macgregor, in his letter to the Secretary to Government, thus speaks of this affair: " I would beg to bring to the notice of his Lordship in Council the gallant and spirited conduct of all the officers and men engaged on this occasion, and particularly that of Captain Sotheby, R.N., whose performance of the very arduous duty of escorting that large fleet up so rapid and difficult a river, with one bank crowned with forts, manned by the enemy, has been such as to merit the very best acknowledgments that I can bestow. The crowning exploit of attacking and capturing the strongest fort on the river with his handful of men, will recommend itself at once to the notice of his Lordship in Council."

After taking Chanderpore, the fleet proceeded up the river as far as Nourainie Ghat, where it arrived on the evening of the 19th. Here there was another fort, and 4000 or 5000 rebels in the vicinity. Four or five miles further on, Jung Bahadoor was encamped near Gai Ghat, with 8000 or 9000 troops and artillery. A fruitless attempt had been made by the Maharajah to effect a lodgment of troops across the river, prior to the arrival of our force; but, owing to some mismanagement, which brought down the fire of the enemy from the opposite bank, terrifying and scaring the workmen employed at the rafts, the attempt was abandoned. It was therefore thought advisable to cross that night without delay, lest the enemy, hearing of the arrival of the fleet, should come down in force, and give serious opposition. At nine, P.M., the boats were ready, and all arrangements were made for the crossing; and by ten o'clock the men of the Naval Brigade, who had formed the escort, with two twelve-pounder howitzers, five companies of Gorkhas, and the detachment of Sikhs, landed on the opposite bank. The other two guns of the naval artillery were brought down to the left bank of the river, a little below the fort, to cover the landing party; and notwithstanding a long march that day of twenty miles under a burning sun,. and the men having the fatiguing duty of pulling the guns along a heavy sandbank, and wading up to their waists in water, they performed it with their usual good spirit and zeal; and about midnight the village and fort were seized and occupied. Arising from the difficulty of getting accurate information, it was quite impossible to ascertain the strength of the garrison; and therefore the fort was approached with all the caution that would be required with a formidable enemy in the entrenchments. On approaching the fort a still and solemn silence prevailed throughout the ranks. Not a word was heard. They crept from the adjacent woods into the bamboo jungle which usually surrounds these Oudh forts. Slow and cautious was the advance. Next the rifle-pits were passed. A fire was found in front of the gate, and a native asleep on a charpoy (native bed). He was seized by the throat and passed to the rear before he was allowed to speak. The inner entrance was then found, and being open, the troops passed up the narrow causeway which led to the interior of the fort; and not until then was the discovery made that it had been abandoned by the rebels. If this had been known previously, the landing might have been effected without any delay, and the combatants would have been saved the disappointment of having no one to encounter. With the sod for a bed, and the trees for a canopy, the troops waited for the events of the ensuing day.

Early in the morning of the 20th the remainder of the force crossed the river, and every exertion was made to ferry over spare ammunition and other stores with the utmost speed, under the indefatigable energy of Lieutenant Grant, R.N. And in the forenoon the Sarun field force was augmented by a brigade of Gorkhas with six guns. About noon a few musket-shots were heard, which causing an alarm, the assembly was sounded. The men were formed into line, and the gunners stood to their guns. Upon inquiry it was found that the men of the advanced piquet fired upon what they imagined to be a reconnoitring party of the enemy; but turning out to be a false alarm, the troops, who had been greatly fatigued from marching and want of rest, retired to the shelter of the tope until the afternoon, when they were again ordered under arms.

About two o'clock, the force, including the Naval Brigade and four guns, with Royal Marines, 190 men, 44 Sikhs, and 1300 Gorkhas with six guns, attached to which were European artillery sergeants, left the camp, and marched six or seven miles to attack the rebels at the village of Phoolpore, three companies of Gorkhas and a few men of the Naval Brigade having been left to protect the baggage. Notwithstanding the fatigue of the previous day, and the absence of rest the previous night, still the men marched cheerfully and willingly to meet the enemy for the second time on the soil of Oudh. With this prospect before them, all fatigue and want of rest was forgotten.

By the order of Colonel Rowcroft, the line was formed about half a mile beyond our camping-ground: the Ramdhul regiment of Gorkhas was on the left of the line, the Naval Brigade with four guns was in the centre, and the other Gorkhas, with a light field-battery of six guns, were on the right. The Gorkhas were commanded by their own regimental officers; but to each regiment there was one or more European officer in military charge, who held a very anomalous and by no means agreeable position, not being able to give orders, and being obliged often to submit to much inconvenience from their resistless determination to have their own way. The line then advanced, a detachment of Royal Marines under Lieutenant Pym, and Sikhs under Lieutenant Burlton, being pushed forward on the right, in skirmishing order, and two companies of Gorkhas on the left. Having passed several topes and hamlets without meeting with the insurgents, the line continued advancing as far as the village of Phoolpore; which being left on our right rear, and coming within range of their guns, a sharp and sudden cannonade from the rebels soon pointed out their position. They were posted, as usual, near and in a wood, with broken ground and some high crops in front, while their left rested on the river.

The enemy kept up a very heavy fire for some time from four or five guns, which was quickly responded to by the naval artillery under Lieutenant Turnour and by the guns of the Nepalese; but among the Gorkhas no little confusion ensued. It is said to be their custom in action to rally round their guns. This probably arises from the fact that they place more confidence in their long range than in the close quarters required for the use of the bayonet. Without pretending to account for the fact with any degree of accuracy, it is, however, quite certain that in a short time after the commencement of the action few of them were to be seen in the line—in fact, they disappeared. Those on the left went over to the right, where the Gorkha Brigadier was commanding; and after the first violence of the fire had a little abated, they might be seen returning stealthily to their ranks.

The scene among the elephants which carried the spare ammunition might be regarded as amusing, if it had occurred on another less serious occasion. They roared and snorted, blowing with their great proboscis, the mahouts, or drivers, using every effort to bring back and quiet them. They kicked them behind the ears as they sat astride on their necks, and hammered them violently on the skull with a great iron spike to bring them to a sense of duty; they abused them, calling them insulting epithets, and by turns coaxed them with endearing terms—but all in vain ; two, after a little time, between the influence of alternate abuse and entreaty, became quieted and accustomed to the noise of the cannon, while the third ran off the field, and no exertion could induce him to return.

The enemy were supposed to be about

2000 or 2500, with a few troops of cavalry and five guns, under the command of Gholam Hossein and Ali Hyder, of whom the latter was wounded in the action. After an hour the infantry gave way, and the cavalry were not long in following. The Marines and Sikhs on the right pushed on in skirmishing order, advancing with such rapidity and daring, that upon coming sufficiently close to the enemy at their guns to be recognised, they cried out, "Gora log," (white people)! and ran, leaving their guns on the field, which the Marines, under command of Lieutenant Pym, immediately captured, passing by the first, and then coming up with the second, which was abandoned and burst; the explosion of which, as well as its tumbril, probably gave rise to the idea that it was destroyed by a shot from a gun directed by Jung Bahadoor. They then crept round, concealed by the bank of the river, nearing the enemy unobserved, until they came within a hundred yards; when a Gorkha officer ran up, violently vociferating that they were firing on the Gorkhas, and using threatening gestures to a Marine who had just discharged his rifle. But, on getting rid of this troublesome messenger, Sergeant Butler and the Marines rushed at the gun, taking it, it may be said, almost at the point of the bayonet, the enemy sticking tenaciously to their post, the last man not having retired ten yards, when they ran up breathless, and gallantly turning it against the former possessors, fired several rounds of grape on the flying foe. One of the Sikhs instantly struck a light, and the limber supplied a port-fire. The Gorkhas then quickly coming up, laid claim to the credit of capturing the guns which the Marines and Sikhs left behind, and triumphantly paraded them in camp the following day.

The Marines by this time got far in advance on the right in the pursuit, well supported by the detachment of Sikhs, who never held back when there was an enemy in front. The seamen likewise on the left pushed forward, leaving the Gorkha Brigade, with their artillery, in the rear; while the Ramdhul regiment of Gorkhas, which had, after four months' intercourse, fostered a degree of intimacy with our men, kept up well, and in company with the naval artillery and seamen under Captain Sotheby, R.N., pursued the enemy until the shades of evening rendered further pursuit impossible. We then returned to the tope about a mile in advance of the village of Phoolpore, where the Gorkha Brigade, not willing to march back to camp, seven miles distant, settled down to bivouac for the night, lighting their fires and making themselves as happy as the circumstances would allow. The Naval Brigade returned to camp at ten o'clock at night, where the tents were ready pitched to receive them. Several of the enemy were killed, but the number could not be accurately ascertained, while our casualty list was very small. There were only a few of the Europeans wounded, and of the Gorkhas only one was killed, and very few wounded. In addition to those of the enemy found on the field after the action, their comrades were seen to be assiduous in picking up their wounded men, putting them in carts, and carrying them off the field in their flight; some of them, it was reported, were subsequently found dead on the road. The steadiness and coolness of the seamen under Lieutenant Radcliffe, while the fire was hottest, and round shot falling about, and tearing up the ground in every direction, were admirable; and the only way to account for the small number of casualties, was the rapid advance, by which the enemy lost their range; they finding it to their advantage to play at long balls, while our men found the nearer they got to the enemy the safer they were.

Thus ended the action at Phoolpore, in which, after a contest of an hour, the rebels, who had occupied the right bank of the Gogra for some days, in the presence of Jung Bahadoor's army, were overthrown and dispersed. Three guns were taken, and camp equipage was destroyed, and "by the skilful dispositions that were made, and the admirable manner in which they were carried out,"* complete success followed, and the passage of the river was secured.

This was the only action in which I have seen the Gorkhas make a "Kookrie charge." The kookrie is a crooked-bladed knife, varying from twelve to fifteen inches long, and from being sharp at the point, it spreads out towards the centre of the blade, perhaps to two or two-and-a-half inches broad. It is a considerable weight, and with it they who are expert in its use can deal a deadly blow.

---

* Brigadier Macgregor's despatch.

It is protected by a scabbard, and worn at the side, in the Kamarband, or girdle. They place implicit confidence in its use, and can, it is said, sever the head from the body of an ox with a single blow. And from being the national arms of Nepaul, their greatest chiefs wear them, mounted either with gold or silver, and sometimes splendidly adorned with jewels. When preparing for the charge, the line forms in open order, either two or four deep, and with a fierce yell, brandishing their formidable weapons high in mid air, they rush wildly on. After the first sharp volley was over, and the enemy had retired to a little distance, our line advanced, and the Ramdhul regiment was persuaded to try the effect of a charge through some thick crops and a tope where it was possible a few of the enemy might have loitered behind; but on dashing on, brandishing their kookries, and uttering piercing yells, they approached the wood, fired their muskets, and entered, but found the enemy had gone.

For two days following the action, the seamen and marines of the Naval Brigade were employed in constructing a bridge of boats; but, on its completion, instead of being permitted to proceed with the Nepalese troops to the siege of the capital, they were the first to cross it, making a retrograde movement into the district of Goruckpore. This naturally produced much disappointment among the men, which was not altogether allayed by the assurance that was given that the post of honour was, on this occasion, in the rear, for that 37,000 rebels were reported to be in the vicinity of Fyzabad, while there were not 1500 troops left behind to meet them. If disparity of numbers is calculated to render a post honourable, so great a disproportion has a fair claim to distinction. There was, however, to meet the odds, that "moral force which constitutes two-thirds of the strength of armies," augmenting the influence of the few, and magnifying their indomitable courage. Much correspondence had been kept up regarding the destinies of the Naval Brigade. At one time it was intended that it should go to Lucknow, and share the honour of its fall; but, as was justly remarked, it is impossible for every corps to be in the front, no matter how much they may desire it; some must be left behind, and, in addition to this inevitable necessity, there was another difficulty arising from the inconvenience of parading European troops, especially so small a force, with a large Nepalese army. Their prejudice against the slaying of the ox is very strong; I have heard, and have every reason to believe it true, that the officers in military charge with Jung's army never had beef on their mess table while in his camp. Their food was confined to fowls and mutton, and even for the few days that we were together, disputes arose, notwithstanding the excessive caution invariably used. A serious quarrel was more than once imminent. When only two regiments were with us, there was little difficulty in keeping the peace; but on the arrival of the Maharajah's army, with his still larger body of camp followers, it became troublesome work. Several frivolous complaints were made with reference to the killing of oxen for food for our men, and on one occasion our noble allies cut adrift the oxen which were crossing the river for the force, suspecting that they were intended for food; and one of them in a fury drew his kookrie in a most threatening manner on one of our men. Consequently, all things considered, it might have been injudicious to have gone with such troublesome allies on a long march.

CHAPTER VI.

Jung Bahadoor's Durbar—Nepalese Uniform—March to Kuptangunge—Character of the Country—The Fort of Belwa—The Bengal Yeomanry Cavalry join our Force—The Attack on Belwa.

FEBRUARY 24th.—The Naval Brigade re-crossed the river and encamped on the left bank. In the afternoon the Maharajah Jung Bahadoor held a durbar, or levee, which many of the officers attended. His Excellency's tent was in a small court-yard formed by a wall of canvas (if canvas can receive that name). His reception was most polite, and his manner gracious. His personal appearance was attractive for an Eastern. His features were small, his complexion sallow, and his expression shrewd and intelligent. He was attended by his principal officers, who, as well as himself, were richly attired. His costume was plain white—not a Parisian, but an Eastern fashion; and on his head he wore a magnificent tiara of diamonds and emeralds of great value. His brothers, who were present, were dressed in gaudy splendour, presenting a striking contrast to the simple magnificence of his own costume; their coats were not only embroidered, but the breast and collar appeared to be a mass of wrought gold. Others seemed to be richly attired according to their rank. One of them wore trousers, not, as is sometimes seen in Europe, with a gold stripe, but entirely covered or interwoven with gold. Their tiaras, with a bird-of-paradise plume waving in front, varied in the degree of their magnificence; but none of them was equal to their chief's.

On coming out to meet us after entering the courtyard, each was introduced, and in a truly English style greeted us by shaking hands. On being conveyed to his tent, the fashion at his durbar, we were informed, was neither to uncover the head, nor to take off the shoes. The chief sat at the upper end of the tent; and along one side sat his general officers, while on the side opposite sat the officers who came to make their salaams, and whose plain campaigning uniform could not compete with the splendour of the Nepalese. After having sat for a short time, and among other topics making some inquiries about the Baltic and Black Sea, and the war in the Crimea, with which Jung seemed to be tolerably acquainted, we all rose up to retire. The conversation was of course confined to the senior officers, and those also who could speak Hindostanee; nor was it of long duration or very varied: the other officers of his court not offering any remark. On our departure the Maharajah escorted us to the door of his enclosed court-yard, and shaking hands, we bade him farewell. It is not at all improbable that both he and his companions washed their hands after intercourse with the Feringhee allies. Next day, the 25th, the force marched from Gai Ghat, and in three marches arrived at Kuptangunge, which was only two marches from Fyzabad.

The first intention was to halt at the village of Bustee, which being in a central position, and only forty-four miles from the town of Goruckpore, relief might be given to that town if attacked. On further consideration it was deemed more desirable to make two marches in advance of this position, that the peaceable might be inspired with confidence, and the rebelliously disposed with a salutary fear, and thus the district in some degree becoming settled, the hands of the civil authorities might be strengthened.

The field force still consisted of the Naval Brigade and two regiments of Gorkhas 500 strong each; but, unfortunately, the

Ramdhul regiment, which had been with us for some months, and upon which some dependence could be placed, was exchanged for one composed of raw recruits which had never seen a shot fired.

On the 2nd of March the force marched to Amorha, distant twelve or thirteen miles from Fyzabad, and pitched the camp in an open maidan, or plain. The country here is very much the same as that throughout Goruckpore; perfectly level, like the surface of a lake. Not a rise is to be seen in any direction, except where a tank has been sunk for the reception of water, and the clay which has been excavated forms an embankment of a few feet high. Small villages and hamlets are scattered here and there, attached to the house of a Zemindar, which is somewhat superior to the others in structure and size; while topes of mango-trees, a quarter or half a mile apart, give an air of luxuriance and greenness in the hot season, when, after the crops are cut, the arable land looks brown and barren until the first shower again converts it into verdure and productiveness. In some villages may be seen the house of a Rajah, or Ranee, *i.e.*, the reigning widow of a Rajah, which, from its size, and perhaps from an attempt at bastions and earthworks, gives the idea that it contains some articles of value to defend.

It is a religious act among the Hindoos to plant a tope, and dig a well. The inventor of that superstition acted on the soundest principles of worldly wisdom; for the former, in the fruit season, yields support to multitudes of the poor, while its foliage gives shelter to travellers from the broiling heat of the sun; and the latter being the source of productiveness in the irrigation of the fields, are easily sunk in every direction; and the ground being saturated by the deluges that fall during the rains, water is procured near the surface in the dry season, and is conveyed by little canals over every yard of ground.

On the arrival of the field force at Amorha, a messenger was sent to Colonel Rowcroft to say that the fort at Belwa, seven miles further on, was occupied by the enemy; and hearing that they were not numerous, urging him to send a party at once to take it before the garrison was reinforced. Belwa is only seven or eight miles distant from Fyzabad, which was once the seat of government of Oudh, and still, in importance, is a city, second only to Lucknow. The rebels occupied this city in great force, improving, by order of the Begum, the old fortifications by which it was surrounded. After the Nepalese army had taken possession of, and passed through Goruckpore, one of their brigades was ordered in advance to the village of Belwa, as a sort of corps of observation; but, by reason of the proximity to Fyzabad, it was found necessary to throw up earthworks, and construct an entrenched camp in such an advanced and exposed position, and in the presence of a numerous enemy. Earthworks were immediately thrown up, and a deep ditch was dug all round, under the superintendence of a skilful European engineer officer, who no doubt selected the best and most defensible ground; and in a short time a fort, with a strong and spacious Pucca building in the centre, rose into view. It was occupied by the Gorkhas only a very short time, until Jung's army was on the point of crossing the Gogra. He then sent orders to his Brigadier to march forthwith to join him. A large quantity of grain and supplies was in the fort at the time, for which there was no means of obtaining carriage in such haste. The Bengal Yeomanry Cavalry were some miles distant, and in six hours could have come to take possession of the fort and supplies, which they could have held until reinforcements arrived; but Jung's orders were urgent—there was not sufficient time to destroy the entrenchments—his officers have too great a regard for their heads to make any delay in obeying his orders, and the European officers in military charge do not seem to have had much influence in making any alteration in the movement. Finally, the camp was struck; the works were left intact; they marched to join Jung: and scarcely had it been evacuated two hours, when a body of the rebels, who had all along been hovering about like vultures round a carcase, entered into undisputed possession of the fort and grain. The earthworks were strengthened, four guns were planted in position on the bastions, and on the approach of the cavalry, the first intimation of the presence of an enemy was a shot from one of their guns.

This information being communicated as the force arrived on the camping ground at

Amorha, and the number of the enemy being reported only 200, the best course to pursue seemed to be an immediate attack before reinforcements could arrive to strengthen the garrison. One hundred and sixty-eight men of the Naval Brigade, with four guns, and 24-pounder rockets, thirty-five Sikhs, and a regiment of Gorkhas, were ordered by Colonel Rowcroft to proceed in the afternoon to Belwa, where they were joined by the Bengal Yeomanry Cavalry, 250 strong. Then three hearty cheers were raised by the new comrades, which were quickly, and with the best of good will, responded to by the jolly tars, who now, for the first time since their military career in India commenced, fell in with troops of their own country and colour. Right well did they know how to appreciate their presence and admire their bravery; and with the best of good will were they encamped together, and in many an action did they meet the enemy side by side during two arduous and trying campaigns.

After the long march of the morning, most of the men of the Naval Brigade got a lift on elephants, and by four o'clock in the afternoon were within a mile of Belwa. A plan of the fort had not been left with the colonel commanding our force, and consequently the nature of the entrenchment and ground was unknown. The number of our Europeans being small, considerable caution and circumspection was required, as any rash or unsuccessful attack, which should place many of our men *hors de combat* might be the means of paralysing our right arm at a time when there was not a European soldier within a hundred miles of us. On nearing Belwa the day was drawing to a close, affording but little hope for active operations. Five o'clock struck before our guns opened fire. It was reconnoitred, and found much stronger than what had been represented; while the defenders turned out to be much more numerous than had been reported. The naval guns threw in shell with great precision for some time; but being only 12-pounder howitzers it would be impossible to make a breach in earthworks with that weight of metal. It was now becoming dark, and to storm it with so small a number of Europeans might result in weakening the only reliable force, especially as our allies did not seem disposed to take part in such an enterprise. Darkness coming on, the force was obliged to retire, and took up their quarters that night in the camp of their new companions in arms, the Bengal Yeoman Cavalry. Next morning, in company with this valiant corps of volunteers, we returned to the camp at Amorha to await the tide of events.

That night and the following day the rebels received large reinforcements. Fyzabad was emptied of them. They flowed in from Nawabgunge, Gondah, and the adjoining districts. They flocked to the green standard, fortunately without having any very clear idea who waved it, or any spirit of cohesion to cement them together in a common cause.

CHAPTER VII.

The Country disaffected—Perilous Position of the Field Force—Destruction of a Village by Elephants—Battle of Amorha—Disparity of Numbers—Rout of the Enemy—Goruckpore saved—Sikhs' looting Propensity.

ON the 4th of March authentic reports were brought in of the many thousands that were gathering, and of fourteen guns that were ready for action. Their leaders interpreted the return from Belwa to the camp on the 2nd, not only as a retreat but as a defeat, and, like a drowning man catching at a straw, made the best use of it to raise the hopes of the supporters of a bad cause, and inspire among the Sepais and disaffected visions of future triumph. It required little to excite them to action, and they seldom seemed to be downcast after a defeat. They took it quite as a matter of course, and were ready for another attempt a few days afterwards notwithstanding the certainty of a similar result. But on this occasion they rejoiced in a fine chance. They knew well that our entire force, including sick, did not amount to more than 1500; and therefore with more confidence they assembled their hosts to the battle.

This part of the country was utterly disaffected. It was visible in the look and demeanour of every villager; they were nearly all tinged with rebellion, and the reward that was held out to our force for not obtaining permission to march to the scene of action in the front at Lucknow, on the ground that the rear would be the post of honour, that there the rebels would be numerous, seemed now on the point of being realized.

Considering the multitudes that could be collected from the adjacent frontier of Oudh and the paucity of the Sarun Field Force, there was much peril in this isolated position. There was not a European soldier within a hundred miles of us or more, and if a rising had been effected in our rear, and the ammunition and supplies which were on the road had been cut off, the force would not have been in an enviable position; but by excellent arrangements these contingencies were provided for and guarded against. A rifle-pit was dug round the camp, which had been pitched in an open plain. A thick jungle in our front was cut down, and a village cleared away, the walls of which were knocked down by a dozen of elephants, who expeditiously performed the work of demolition. The obedience and docility of these animals is surprising. The walls of the houses were two or two and a half feet thick, and built of strong, tenacious, and compact mud. At the bidding of the mahout the elephant would push it with his ponderous forehead, throwing the weight of his body into the shove. Sometimes, if this failed, he would open his wide mouth and bite the top of the wall and pull down loosened and detached pieces with his trunk, and then, with the wall thus mutilated and weakened, he would try the pressure of his skull again, levelling a village with marvellous rapidity. These and other arrangements being made, we waited the advance of the enemy.

The camp was struck at two o'clock next morning, the 5th; the tents were packed and the baggage-carts were loaded, so as to put all the *impedimenta* into as small a space as possible, for protection in a neighbouring village, and that as few troops as possible might be required for a guard, lest the main body should be weakened.

The rebels' spies informed them that we were in full retreat, and on hearing tidings so flattering to their hopes, their courage rose several degrees, and prepared for a speedy pursuit. About seven o'clock, after a wearisome and tedious delay, the troops having been under arms for five hours, and at work nearly all night, a report was brought in by the corindar of a Ranee who resided about a mile from our camp, that the enemy was going to attack Mhaun Sing, that he had just returned from their camp at Belwa, and that they had no intention of coming down on us that day. A report coming from so respectable an authority as the Ranee's head man, gained implicit credence, and orders were issued to repitch the camp, which were on the point of being carried out, when another report came in of a contradictory character. A patrol of cavalry was sent out to reconnoitre, and returning with tidings that the enemy was advancing, Colonel Rowcroft doubled the strength of the patrol, and ordered the officer in command to obtain further information. All hands stood to their arms.

The force moved out of camp about seven o'clock, and having taken up a position about half a mile to the west of the village of Amorha, formed line. The Naval Brigade and four guns were in the centre across the road, under the command of Captain Sotheby, R.N. The two Gorkha regiments were on the right and left of the Naval Brigade, in military charge of Captains Brooks, Berkley, and Macgregor. The Sikh detachment under Lieutenant Burlton, was on the left of the Gorkhas; and the Bengal Yeomanry Cavalry, one squadron on the right of the line under Captain Chapman, and the other on the left under Major Richardson, covering both flanks.

It was at first conjectured that the report might have its origin from a party of the enemy being sent out to plunder the neighbouring villages; but soon their bugle-calls were heard, first sounding the halt and then the advance, which put it beyond all doubt that they were approaching. Our line remained steady in position, anxiously awaiting the moment when the enemy should come within range. Their bugle-calls were heard nearer and nearer, and they soon showed themselves in great force. They deployed into line, extending right and left to a great distance, probably a mile or more each way, overlapping our flanks, and threatening to overwhelm our small force. They pushed forward a cloud of skirmishers; there was no lack of drilled troops; they came on in admirable order, as if confident of success. Looking on these advancing masses from the rear of the line, our troops appeared a handful of men compared with this approaching wave crested with bayonets.

The naval guns under Lieutenant Turnour opened fire from the centre, and the enemy with ten guns commenced a heavy and furious cannonade on our line. This was kept up obstinately on both sides for some time. The skirmishers were thrown out, and the order was given, "The line will advance;" an order that was never rescinded, and that was promptly carried out, until the whole force was driven off the field. Their line was so extended, that when their centre was driven back they seemed, on their extreme right, to be quite unconscious of the fact, and marched down deliberately and leisurely towards our camp. This movement being observed, Colonel Rowcroft sent orders to Major Richardson, commanding the left squadron, to detach a troop, or, if necessary, with the squadron, to charge and clear out the enemy. This was gallantly and effectually carried out by Major Richardson, well supported by Captain Brooks of the 1st Light Cavalry, with two companies of Gorkhas. The cavalry, in their impetuosity, dashed forward at a hand-gallop, riding through a Jheel (a shallow lake, or sheet of water), no impediment retarding their advance or assuaging their ardour. They soon came upon the enemy, driving them back, cutting up and killing a number of them, and dispersing them thoroughly. Several horses were shot or wounded, but fortunately no trooper received any serious injury, some having received slight wounds or a hair-breadth escape. Many a hand-to-hand fight might be described, when a Sepai, despairing of his chance of escape, turned round, stood his ground, and fought fiercely with his mounted antagonist, using either his bayonet or butt-end of his musket, as best suited his taste; and sometimes he would make a cut at the horses' legs with his tulwar as he passed, which was a favourite trick with those who were unable to make a defence.

After the first fierce cannonade was over, the roar of the artillery began to subside. They then seemed to consider, they then halted—then wavered. It is fatal to delay under such circumstances; when it comes to that, a dash is sure to gain the day. From the first moment they were observed to waver, no time was to be lost; a rapid and decisive blow was to be struck then or never, if complete success was to be ensured. Colonel Rowcroft immediately ordered a party of Naval Riflemen to reinforce the Royal Marine skirmishers, while he ordered Captain Chapman with his squadron to advance, inclining to the right, and charge the enemy's Sowars and infantry: at the same time orders were sent to the Gorucknath regiment of Gorkhas to advance at the charge. All this time the first order issued was attended to by the Naval Brigade, which continued advancing upon the multitudes in front, and never halted to draw breath except when they came within easy range for a discharge of grape. Then they unlimbered the guns, fired as many rounds as the retreating multitude would wait to receive; then limbering up, would gallop the guns more like horse than foot artillery, and when within range, would again unlimber and discharge as many rounds as the time admitted; limbered up and galloped on, chasing them with a speed, and working their guns with an activity, truly surprising.

Among the number of guns that were taken, one, from its proximity to the enemy, afforded a peculiar opportunity to be turned against themselves. Lieutenant Grant, Mr. Shearman the engineer, a seaman named Jesse Ward, another seaman, and Lord Charles Scott, midshipman, rushed forward, captured the gun, and loaded it from the contents of its own limber; but having no portfire, a rifle was discharged with the muzzle to the vent, which answered the purpose, giving the enemy the benefit of grape out of their own piece of ordnance.

Captain Chapman, in the meantime, with his squadron made a most gallant charge, routing the left wing, and scattering the multitude. The enemy now no longer hesitated; their centre was driven back, and both wings shaken; the Sowars (Native Cavalry) were in rapid retreat, and the infantry soon followed. The combined movement of the troops, the formidable charge of the cavalry, the steady advance of the Naval Brigade, soon shattered the whole line of the enemy. They abandoned eight guns, which were left unspiked, seven were taken on the field, one could not be found. They varied in size from an 18-pounder to a 9-pounder, 6-pounders, and guns of smaller calibre, with gun-carriages and seven limbers complete, well stored with ammunition, and drawn by bullocks, which were also left on the field, as well as a cart with 25,000 musket-balls.

The pursuit now commenced. For six miles the rebels were driven from tope to tope, and from village to village. Wherever they took shelter, from thence they were speedily expelled, until our horses and men, completely worn out with fatigue, and exhausted with heat, were obliged to halt. Once they made a short stand, keeping up a fire from the only two guns that they succeeded in carrying off, and discharging, as they did from the commencement of the engagement, a perfect hailstorm of musket-balls. Here we lost an officer of the Naval Brigade, Mr. Fowler, and one Gorkha, a private; but the effective fire of the guns, the steady advance of the line, and the right squadron moving forward, threatening another charge, soon drove them out of sight.

Considering the small number of European troops* which were available to meet such an overwhelming force, no doubt our

---

* Gorkhas, 850; Bengal Yeomanry Cavalry, 200; marines, 32; naval column, 140; 4 naval guns; 39 Sikhs. Total, 1261.

position was that of considerable danger; but, as British seamen and soldiers always do, they faced it with a daring and determination adequate to dispel the danger; they gallantly dashed forward, amidst showers of ball, and after pushing forward two or three miles farther, they began to suffer so much from fatigue and heat, that they were obliged to halt. Having been up nearly the whole previous night, and during the action marching through heavy ground and thick cultivation, they halted for a short time to rest, and then returned to the camp.

The action commenced at half-past eight in the morning, and was terminated at half-past twelve. In four hours the enemy, who were reported to be 4000 Sepais, 10,000 irregular troops, 300 Sowars, and ten guns, were completely defeated and routed by 1261 men and four guns, with a severe loss, in killed and wounded, of about 500.

The Sepais were of the 1st, 10th, 53rd, and 56th Regiments of Native Infantry, 5th Regiment Gwalior Contingent, and 2nd Oudh Police Force. The Nazim Mahomed Hussein, and the Rajahs of Gondah and Churdah, and other chiefs, were present on elephants, but were said to have left early in the action. On the return of the force it was found that the few men who could be spared to guard the captured guns, had brought them into camp; and, to our no small satisfaction, we saw them safely parced, and among the spoils were limbers in good serviceable condition, which formerly were the property of the Honourable East India Company.

Thus the teeth of the tiger were drawn for that time, as the natives of India without guns venture to do but little, the noise of their cannon considerably raising their courage. In half an hour the camp was repitched, and the troops got rest and refreshment. By striking the tents and packing the baggage, the eyes of the rebels were completely blinded. Their spies told them we were retreating; and thus, being prepared for a pursuit and a speedy victory, they came on full of confidence, until, to their no small surprise and chagrin, never expecting to see so small a force showing so bold a front, they found a little phalanx that never gave way ready to receive them. It was marvellous to see so great a host chased away as if panic-stricken by the audacity of such a handful, facing about when they expected to see them turn right about face, and marching away. Some of the seamen would jocularly say to their comrades, as they were " bolting" off, " What are these rascals bolting away for? If they would only come on with sticks, they must have beat us." But they were deficient in true patriotism, they were deficient in *esprit de corps*, and their foul deeds deprived them of the favour of the Ruler of armies. An educated Hindoo, who was too wise and far-seeing to sympathize with the Sepais, remarked to me that "God fought for us, and would fight for us again;" and his providence and intervention in our favour was duly acknowledged next morning, when, at a parade of the troops, thanksgivings were offered to the "Giver of all victories" for this great and signal success, and his providential care in permitting so little loss to be sustained on our side compared with that of the enemy. Of the Naval Brigade we had to lament the loss of one officer killed; fourteen or fifteen men were wounded; of the Gorkhas, one was killed, and several were wounded; the cavalry had two horses killed, and several were wounded; several troopers also were wounded, but none were killed; many, as may easily be imagined, had narrow escapes. The naval guns would naturally be a mark for the enemy to shoot at; and therefore would have a fair share of their attention. Every gun or limber was struck, once or oftener, by grape or round shot, but fortunately none were disabled. Some of the Jacks, seeing the balls falling about, striking their guns or their limbers without wounding a man, said, in their own phraseology, acknowledging a superhuman Providence, "Well, Bill, this almost makes me superstitious." The shot fell fast and thick, ricochetting along the ground in every direction. A heavy fire of musketry was constantly kept up; but fortunately the failing of the Sepais in firing too high was again our safety. It was soon found that the nearer to the enemy, the greater was the security, the balls passing clear over the heads of the troops in the line, their whiz being the only inconvenience. Notwithstanding, it was evident, from the manner in which they retreated, that they were trained soldiers. This was not altogether proved by their uniform, however, which was rather "the worse for the wear." Some of them had cross-belts and red jackets, muskets, and bayonets; some had the uniform jacket without the trousers, and some the trousers without the jacket; some wore the jacket with the regulation musket, and some were reduced to the necessity of using native arms and dispense with uniform altogether. In fact, their tailors evidently did not supply them with the latest military cut.

Taking into consideration the comparative numbers, this battle was singularly successful, and may justly be regarded as having saved the rich fertile plains "of Goruckpore from a second inundation"* of rapacious harpies, who, no doubt, would have been aided by numerous local Baboos and Zemindars, if they had succeeded in their plans.

---

* Brigadier Rowcroft's despatch.

By the excellent arrangements that were made the numbers of our men appeared to be greater than they really were; so that when their leaders urged the Sepais to try the fortune of war again, they replied that they had been deceived already by being told that the European troops were only 400, while in the field they met the "Gora log" on the right flank, on the left flank, in the centre, and everywhere; thus paying a compliment to the activity with which our force moved, magnifying their numbers, and giving them a ubiquitous appearance. On their return to Fyzabad their friends laughed at them for being beaten by so small a force, and they were shamed into making promises (as we learned from the reports of the spies) to retrieve their character—promises which were never fulfilled; and gave out that they had bound themselves by an oath to attack the Feringhees and not to run away. They were resolved, however, to make some one suffer for the defeat, and consequently they hung their spy who told them that our force was retiring, and next day, the spy that told us a similar story about them, met a similar fate. He was convicted of a peculiarly aggravated offence: he was a corindar in the employment of a Ranee, who, living close to our camp, was professedly on friendly terms with our Government; he brought information that he had just come from the enemy's camp, and that they had not the least intention of attacking us that day, but were going in an opposite direction to punish Maun Sing. And this intelligence he conveyed in order to put us off our guard at the very hour that he knew they were marching down towards our camp. He was accordingly convicted, and paid the penalty with death, which he met with perfect indifference, adjusting the noose round his neck with his own hands, and leaping from the back of the elephant on which he had been conveyed to the place of execution.

Among the Gorkhas who were wounded, one was disabled for life by the loss of his leg; and becoming unfit for service, he was at once struck off the rolls of his regiment without receiving pay or pension. No care was bestowed on him, and he would have been left houseless and unable to earn a livelihood in a country far from his home, if a subscription had not been raised for him in camp to defray his expenses to Nepaul, and supply him with food by the way. It is not a matter of surprise when men are compelled to serve, and being wounded or disabled, are cast off by the Government of their country, that they should shun the risk which accompanies bravery, and keep out of harm's way as much as they can. And this failing seemed to attach as much to their officers as to their men; the higher they rise in rank being supposed to do the least; exertion, which is incompatible with the dignity of the senior, being confined to the junior. The detachment of Sikhs were as forward as usual, but their natural instinct for plunder is surprisingly strong. At Lucknow they are reputed to have got the lion's share. They seemed to have been a privileged class in that way; at any rate, their great success kept them in a good humour, and no doubt rendered them well satisfied with our service. There are numerous stories about our men picking up some article of trifling value in many places which have been taken, perhaps emerging from a house with a clock under his arm, or a few silk handkerchiefs, or a brass lota; while the Sikhs, looking on perfectly regardless would wait until they had finished, and then go systematically to work in quest of rupees and gold mohurs. They knew the native's habit of hiding treasure, either built up in a wall or buried under the floor; and by sprinkling water about, discovered the spot where it dried up the quickest, and then speedily disentombed cash and other valuables. On the fifth, as they were in pursuit of the fugitive rebels, some of them could not resist their favourite propensity. It is not sanctioned by the service, but it is a difficult matter to stop it. One was seen with a small bundle on his back as he marched through the high standing crops. By degrees it got bigger and bigger. He would lay it down now and again, fire off his musket, and renew his load. At last he got a lump on his back like a camel. The protuberance that was small in the beginning, by means of the articles accumulated in the route, had swollen to a considerable bulk, like an evil rumour, which increases in size every time it is rehearsed.

Never until now had the Naval Artillery an opportunity of being thoroughly equipped. Limbers and spare ammunition-wagons being captured in abundance, a selection might be made to meet the requirements of the battery. By the incessant industry of Mr. Burton, the ship's carpenter, the battery which took the field in the first action, labouring under the disadvantages of a very inefficient equipment, soon presented the appearance of one efficient for any service.

The Gorkhas seemed quite proud of their achievements in the action, and said that the Brigadier had a lucky star, and that when they went into action with him, victory was the sure result, that their loss was trifling, and their casualties few.

During the time these two regiments were brigaded with the "Pearl's" men they were on excellent terms, and Brigadier Rowcroft, when acknowledging their services, returned thanks at the same time to Captain Sotheby, the officers and men, "who, with their guns," he said, "were his mainstay in the action, and most valuable to him at all times;" a compliment which was again repeated by the Commander-in-Chief, Sir Colin Campbell, who, in his letter of thanks, noticed more particularly the " gallantry of the Bengal Yeomanry Calvary, and the bravery and steadiness of the Naval Brigade."

CHAPTER VIII.

Constant Alarms—A Fort constructed—The Rebels Reinforced—Arrival of the left Wing of H.M. 13th Light Infantry—The Hot Season—Camp Routine—Action near Tilga—Charge of the Bengal Yeomanry Cavalry—The Westerly Winds.

For several days after the combat, the force was constantly on the alert, expecting to be attacked again. On the following Thursday and Tuesday, being regarded by them as "lucky days," they were more especially expected. The Gorkhas also have their "lucky days." On the 5th instant they were confident of success, even those on the sick list strained a point to bear arms. Their lucky days, however, passed away, and no Sepais appeared. Probably if this action had been less successful, or if fewer guns had been captured, they might have tried it again.

It was well known to the experienced East India officers that a bold front was the best security for success; and being convinced of the danger of the slightest appearance of weakness, the trench which had been dug round our camp was filled up, and the camp was pitched in the open plain. However, it was thought advisable to construct a small fort, in which the sick, the spare ammunition, and the baggage might be safely lodged, and requiring only a small guard, the greater part of the force might be free to take the field.

A fort was constructed taking in a small village and the Theseel, which being a strong brick building, made an excellent hospital. On the bastions three of the guns taken from the enemy on the 5th were mounted, rendering it perfectly secure, with a small guard, in the temporary absence of the force.

Their threats were repeated from week to week, more especially on their lucky days. The fueckir, or priest, would urge them to an encounter, and the troops were continually harassed by false alarms, which were as vexatious as a real attack, causing them to be kept out under arms in the sun half the day. Sometimes from an early hour in the morning they would be ordered to stand to their arms, the tents and baggage being packed and lodged in the fort; and forming line in front of the camping ground, they would await an enemy who never appeared. At last, becoming accustomed to these reports, the striking of tents and the packing of baggage were dispensed with; but the men would return from the field in a bad humour at the Sepais not giving them a chance of exchanging a few shots.

The country in our rear was tranquil; fortunately for us, they were void of enterprise. A few thousands might have been detached from the main body, and making a circuit to our rear, have aroused the country into turbulence and confusion; but luckily the rebels managed with singular sagacity to collect a large army without procuring a general, and entertained a disposition to do much more mischief than they knew how to carry out. It was like a body without a head, and having no principle of cohesion, would naturally fall to pieces under a severe blow. They had, however, wonderful vitality, which did not arise from any settled Government, but from being like the troubled sea that cannot rest. Beat them in twenty fights, and the shattered carcase of an army would again reappear, the pieces being collected together, and, like a ghost or dissolving view, would vanish at the first advance of our troops. After two or three engagements, in which they were well beaten, it became a matter of certainty in every subsequent encounter that they would run, and, therefore, the chief object was how to surprise and catch them.

The false alarms continued until the end of April, with two exceptions, when the enemy made their appearance. But it may be asked why the field force remained quiet so long within seven miles of their entrenchments without making some efforts to expel them? This is answered by the fact that our guns, being only 12-pounder howitzers, were not adapted to make a breach in a mud fort; and, secondly, there was a general order that forts should not be attacked without having guns of heavier metal.

The ensign was no sooner unfurled in Lucknow than regiments of fugitives flocked to the standard of the chiefs at Fyzabad, bringing with them cavalry and guns. For some time they hovered around our camp, but evidently reluctant to come to close quarters. The left wing of H.M.'s 13th Light Infantry, 300 strong, under Major Cox, joined our force on the 26th of March, and one Gorkha regiment was sent to Goruckpore. Thus reinforced, the brigade, though numerically weaker, taking into consideration the value of European troops and Enfield rifles, was virtually stronger.

The weather was now becoming exceedingly hot and oppressive, the sun striking fiercely through the tents. The usual routine of camp-life begun to assume a dull chronic form, and was remarkable only for its sameness. At daybreak the reveillée sounded, a general rubbing of eyes and movement of languid limbs ensued, then the assembly sounded, and all hands appeared on the parade-ground in front of the camp. After parade came daily prayers, for the men of the Naval Brigade, which lasted about ten minutes. This custom not being unusual on board a " man-of-war," was continued throughout the campaign. Ball practice or light-infantry drill for an hour or more succeeded, until the sun gave convincing proofs that the men should keep close to their tents during the fiery heat of the day. Nearly all hands began to employ native punca wallas to fan them, and keep the flies at a respectable distance, as well as kitmutgars to wait on them at table; in fact, Jack was a gentleman, "every inch of him."

In order to render our abodes somewhat cooler, the soil under our tents was dug out, and a pit was excavated, three or four feet deep, the superfluous soil being manufactured into a mud wall; and these pits, resembling a sort of mausoleum for the living, although slightly damp, possessed the advantage of a temperature a few degrees cooler.

It would be difficult to say how valuable time was now spent. Sleep was probably the most general and innoxious amusement. Books were a rare commodity. Most of those which were brought up country having disappeared off the face of the earth; and newspapers not being numerous among the men, were regarded as a delicacy. Meal hours were tolerably regular, except when an alarm produced a change in the arrangements. Shortly after the dawn of day, a cup of tea and piece of toast, brought in by the kitmutgar, was presented to the recumbent Sahib with one eye shut, and the other scarcely open, who, overcome with heat and the fatigue of having nothing to do, would mechanically put forth his hand and take hold of the viands, which are called "chota hazri," *i.e.*, little breakfast. Having gone through the duties of the morning, if he should be prone to great exertion, he would take a short walk, or, mounting his horse, would ride for an hour, until common prudence compelled him to take shelter; and then the operations of the day commence. After the toilet is made (with reference to which campaigners are not very particular), breakfast, or " burra hazri," is served up, at hours varying from nine o'clock until eleven or twelve o'clock; the former hour best suiting the demands of a brisk ride on horseback, while the latter would suit those whose exertions were not so violent, and who indulge in the more easy kind of horizontal exercise, in the shape of a stretch on a charpoy.

After breakfast a serious difficulty arises how to pass the day. To go outside the tent is to be grilled; to remain inside, is to be baked. A newspaper arrives by post, which meets with its quantum of abuse for telling nothing new; and if it does contain anything out of the common, it is not believed—it is read, it is abused for its emptiness, it is thrown down, and the worn-out reader falls back exhausted on his couch; perhaps he sleeps, perhaps he only shuts his eyes, trying to lull himself into the belief that he is asleep, until exhausted nature calls again for some support. After the lapse of a few hours, tiffin is announced, and after that there is a general relapse into the former state of temporary inactivity, until the long shadows from the trees are the harbingers of a temperature reduced from 108° to 90° or 95°. Then, recovering from the fatigue of the day, one would mount his horse for a ride, another would walk a mile, or perhaps two. When puncas could not be rigged up in the tents, a native with a huge fan might be seen looking sleek and shining, frightening away the hosts of flies, the plague of which was very great, and producing a breath of artificial air. The attentive punca walla looking as if he needed a cooling himself as much as the Sahib; with this difference, that his wardrobe consisted of only a yard or two of calico, the heat of which gave but little inconvenience.

Darkness having decidedly set in, dinner is announced by the faithful kitmutgar, who coming up with his two hands closed together, and raised in a supplicatory posture, says "kana tayar, hai," dinner is ready. This being concluded, it is followed by tea or coffee, pipes or cigars, winding up with *matériel* of a little stronger nature. After all the affairs of the day are duly discussed—after it is decided that all the rumours of the enemy's attack on the ensuing day is false—after the spies are all voted to be liars—after some argument is warmly kept up by two or more contending belligerents—and after both parties have succeeded in convincing themselves that his opponent is wrong, and that he himself is in the right,—they retire quite satisfied, and turn in for the night. And thus the time is passed until the return of another day brings with it similar cares; and the attentive bearer* approaches respectfully, often lending his aid, by holding the hand of his

---

* A valet.

Sahib, and raising him up from a reclining, to a sitting posture, and, as if to relieve him of all possible exertion, the faithful slave ("gulam"), as the bearer humbly styles himself, having lighted the pipe of his master, would carefully place it in his mouth, and thus relieve him of the trying exertion of lifting his hand for the purpose.

It is difficult for any one who has not experienced it, to conceive the ennui and irksomeness that takes possession of men who pass the hot season in tents in India. The excessive heat, the close confinement to the cotton hut, the difficulty of getting books in camp during these troublous times; the proximity of the enemy, which prevented the possibility of making excursions to a distance, or riding further from camp than a mile or two; the hot winds, which carried clouds of broiling dust; the swarm of flies which crawl about, being too lazy to use their wings except when forcibly compelled, add to the inconvenience and monotony of a tent life at this season of the year.

On the 2nd of April information was received that the rebels at Belwa had been reinforced by 1500 men, and a horsed battery (four 9-pounders, and two 24-pounder howitzers). An attack being probable, there was a sharp look out, and cavalry patrols went reconnoitring. A villager gave information regarding their movements, and among other things he mentioned that, having gathered in all his grain, the produce of his land, the rebels not only took possession of it, but compelled him to bring it to their camp, and then, giving him a beating as a recompense, told him to come next morning if he wanted any more pay. In this way the rebels obtained from their countrymen the sinews of war.

Several thousand of the Lucknow Sepais

having augmented the number of the insurgents about Fyzabad, one of their chiefs whom our force met in many an encounter, Mahomed Hossein, tried to pursuade them to join his standard. To whom they replied that they had had fighting enough with the English already, and dispersed. It was reported that he offered them three months pay if they would beat our force out of the district; but they were unwilling to make the agreement except the pay was given beforehand. Information was also given that some others took him into custody for a week, on account of the arrears that were due; and that subsequently he did not trust himself to their tender mercies, but encamped among his own followers.

At this time sanguine hopes were entertained that another battery of artillery and more troops would be sent to relieve the Naval Brigade and enable them to return to the ship; but the rebels beleaguering Azimghur, detained the troops that were expected to advance into Goruckpore, and thus we were destined to continue in this out-of-the-way corner of the country, isolated from all the rest of the army.

April 17th.—A villager who probably got tired of having his grain looted, brought intelligence that a strong party of insurgents had entered a village not more than three and a half miles from our camp. A cavalry patrol was sent out to reconnoitre, and soon returned, corroborating the report. A detachment was immediately ordered under arms, 100 of the 13th Light Infantry, Captain Chapman's squadron of the Bengal Yeomanry Cavalry, and 200 Gorkhas under the command of Major Cox, and 100 men and two guns of the Naval Brigade, under the command of Captain Sotheby, R.N., left the camp about nine o'clock, A.M., and came up with the rebels near the village of Tilga.

The cavalry, by making a circuit to their rear, took them by surprise, and discovered that their numbers were more than what was represented, having received reinforcements from Belwa, and four guns. The cavalry went sufficiently close to occupy their attention until the infantry and guns arrived. By this time they numbered about 2000 Sepais, besides 1000 Budmashes, a few Sowars, and four guns. Shot and shell were soon sent among them; but the detachment was not sufficiently strong to drive them out of the village. A message was sent to Brigadier Rowcroft for more troops; and in the meantime Major Cox, well knowing the character of John Pandy, managed to draw them out of their hiding-place by a manœuvre which soon had the desired effect. The detachment feigned a retreat; they imagining that the troops were running away, came out yelling and bellowing as if to inflate each other's courage, and seemed disposed to make a desperate effort to drive our party back to camp. But when once out from under cover, the detachment halted, and gave them such a warm reception with rifles and shell, that they soon found themselves safer behind mud walls. The Rajah of Gondah's pundit* here lost his life. On seeing the detachment retire, he discovered that it was one of their "lucky days." He came out of the village, urging the rebels on, and telling them that his predictions were now about to be fulfilled. While thus trying to encourage his people, a stray shot cut him off in the midst of his exhortations, and showed the Rajah the value of his predictions. Having kept this numerous body of rebels at bay for upwards of an hour, Brigadier Rowcroft came out with the rest of the force, and making a detour of a mile and a half to the right, turned the left flank of the enemy. On perceiving the movement,

---

* A wise man, or a sort of soothsayer.

fearing lest their retreat should be cut off, and putting more confidence in the activity of their legs than the precision of their fire, the rebels suddenly retreated, and were pursued by the cavalry. But, in passing by a village, Major Richardson, with a troop of Bengal Yeomanry Cavalry, observed about 300 of the enemy, with one gun, collected under the cover of the houses. The contents of the gun and a volley of musketry were discharged at them; giving the order to charge, he bore down at a gallop, captured the gun, and scattered the rebels. Each Sepai defended himself as best he could, knowing there was no quarter, and that not his days only, but his minutes were numbered; and therefore resolved to sell his life as dearly as he could, and do his utmost to destroy at least one Feringhee. One would bend on one knee and meet the charge with his bayonet; another would reserve the contents of his musket until the trooper was almost sufficiently close to the muzzle that the flash could set his clothes on fire; another would lie down and make a cut at the legs of the horses as they passed; in fact, they stood as well as despair could make them stand. Fifty or sixty of the rebels were cut down, and the nature of the affair may be guessed from the fact that, out of fifty-four, which was the number of the troop, fifteen or sixteen were either killed or wounded. Five horses were killed, five were missing, and seven wounded. Mr. Troup, a cornet, and Brown, a trooper, were killed on the spot; and the Adjutant, Mr. Bridgman, was dangerously wounded; and several others were severely wounded. One gun was taken, and the wheel of another was said to have been destroyed by a shell; but they managed to hide it in a nullah until next morning, when it was conveyed away. The rebels were under the command of a corundar, a sort of premier, of the Rajah of Gondah.

They acknowledged to have lost 200 in killed and wounded—upwards of 80 were known to have been killed. Among the latter was a Sepai who had a few weeks before killed a trooper of the Bengal Yeomanry Cavalry with his own sword. He had been taken prisoner by the trooper, and while bringing him into camp, the Sepai made a grasp at his sword and despatched him; now he was in turn killed, and the sword recovered on the field.

After this action, the little remaining courage of the Sepais cooled down. They made their approaches with marked caution and circumspection. No doubt, in this affair, their chief object was loot. Their looting party bringing out our first detachment, and then the enemy being reinforced, brought out the remainder of the troops, and a general action was the result. The Naval Brigade under Captain Sotheby, and the infantry under Major Cox, attacking them in front, when the flank movement under Brigadier Rowcroft finally obliged them to retire.

It was a most unsatisfactory day for an action; the westerly winds which prevail in some parts of India becoming heated by passing over many hundreds of miles of roasted soil, which has become arid and parched by a burning sun; and while whisking a searching and unbearable dust into every crevice of the human face, added to the fiery rays which are shot from the luminary above, augmented by those reflected by the bleached verdureless soil over which the troops had to march, roasting their eyes, and toasting their skin, may give some idea of the atmosphere, which has been compared to a blast from a furnace, in which an army in the field has to live and fight at this season in India; but the old proverb, "It is an ill wind that blows nobody good," is *à propos* in this case. It is made to produce a refreshingly low temperature in the bungalows of Europeans during the hot season, so that to permanent residents it may be considered an advantage. A kind of door called a tatty, is made of the kuskus, a root which bears a resemblance to dry grass; and being placed in the doorway facing the west, is perpetually kept wet by a cooley throwing water over it; and the hot wind blowing through, produces a cool and refreshing air within, often reducing the thermometer from 100° to 70°.

CHAPTER IX.

Action near Jamoulee—Captain Clarke's' Attack on the Rebels near Bustee—Fatiguing March from Amorha—Taking of Nuggur—Bustee saved.

On the 25th of April, the rebels again moved out of Belwa, and came towards our camp in three columns. The day was as hot and sultry as an April day can be in these parts. They seemed to know, at any rate, what was the best means of weakening European troops; if they failed in doing it by the sword, they adopted a very shrewd method in trying to do it by the climate.

After breakfast a trooper rode in from the advanced cavalry piquet, stating that the enemy were in sight. The bugle sounded to arms, and the horses were yoked to the guns; and a little after eleven o'clock the force marched out to meet them. The line being formed in front of the camp, Brigadier Rowcroft ordered the advance. After proceeding two miles, near the village of Jamoulee, one column of the enemy appeared on our left flank, one in front, and one on the right. The enemy numbered about 4000 men, with four guns. Our line then separated. The left wing, under the command of Major Cox, of H.M. 13th Light Infantry, consisted of a squadron of the Bengal Yeomanry Cavalry, a company and a half of the 13th, and 200 Gorkhas: with two guns, and 100 men of the Naval Brigade under Captain Sotheby. The right wing, under Brigadier Rowcroft, consisted of about an equal number of cavalry and infantry, with two guns and a 24-pound rocket, under Lieutenant Turnour, R.N. The enemy opened fire with shell on the left wing, which, pushing on, caused them to retire; they then moved off more to the left, being still rapidly pursued. The guns under Captain

Sotheby, firing with their usual precision, well supported by the rifles of the seamen under Mr. Ingles, mate, R.N., and the 13th Light Infantry, ably commanded by Major Cox, forced them to retire; but in doing so they inclined towards our left rear, while at the same time the right wing advancing, was unable to get closer to the rebels in front than 1500 yards: 24-pounder rockets, in charge of Lieutenant Grant, were then fired upon them; and these had the desired effect in dispersing the column, which took up a position in a mango-tope. The natives have a salutary dread of the rocket, which they call "Bhan," occasioned probably by a tradition, of which I have heard, attributing the death of the brother of their god Ram to this cause; for, on advancing, we were informed by a villager, that the soubadar in command was the first to "bolt," saying that they could do nothing against Bhan. The others of course soon followed his example. After a short halt to rest the troops, the Brigadier moved over to the left, and joined Major Cox, who was still engaged with another column, which stood their ground in two villages; but by the time the force was again united, the rascals who had run away came on again in front, and on our extreme right, apparently with the intention of threatening our camp. The right wing was obliged to retrace their steps, and when within 1200 yards, the rebels opened fire with shot and shell from a horsed battery, which they kept at a great distance, not wishing to run the risk of losing it at close quarters. Having thus doubled back to the former position, they seemed disposed to keep up a game of long balls. They would not close, or permit our force to close with them; the line advanced, but, as it advanced, they retreated; it pushed on as fast as possible, but the sun was so fierce that the heat was melting. The horses were obliged to drag the guns over very bad, rough ground, enough to destroy more axles and gun-carriages than could easily be replaced; and between marching back and forward, and hunting them from one place to another, from eleven o'clock in the morning until five in the afternoon, the men and horses were so fagged and worn out, that many, both Gorkhas and Europeans, fell down on the road, so that the line was obliged to halt.

This was the most fatiguing day and most unsatisfactory "affair" the Goruckpore field force had engaged in up to this time. The insurgents so distributed their forces as to divide our attention; and keeping at such a distance, that it was quite impossible to get at them; a few were killed by the shell at a very long range; and on our side, although their practice with shot and shell was very good, there was no loss. The shell burst over the heads of the cavalry, and the balls rolled along past the line to the rear among the Dhoolee bearers and camp followers, showing that their battery was managed by experienced gunners; no doubt trained for the service of the Honourable East India Company.

It can scarcely be said that they made an attack: all their manœuvres seemed intended to harass our men, and keep at a sufficient distance to make their escape when closely pressed. When urged to the attack by their leaders telling them that our "guns were small," they remarked that the "spice (shot and shell) was very strong," and thought it safer to keep at a civil distance. If they only desired to allure our men into the sun, and thus weaken the force, the attempt was well managed: but even in this they were disappointed, few of our men suffering much after a night's rest, although the thermometer was up to 105°.

The villagers brought out vessels of water,

and seemed disposed to be friendly; but not much reliance can be placed on their sincerity—very probably they performed the same office for the rebels half an hour before. The Bhisties, or water-carriers attached to the camp, had also plenty to do. These indefatigable servants carry the water in the skin of a sheep turned inside out, called a mussuck, which is placed across their back. The skin is taken off entire without making a longitudinal incision, as is usual in performing this operation. The apertures occasioned by the legs are closed by the skin of each leg being tied tight; and the neck answers for a spout, through which the mussuck is filled, and from which the water is poured out, a greater or less quantity escaping according as it is distended or compressed.

On the following day, April 26th, news was brought in that during the affair of the previous day a body of rebels had started up twenty-two miles in our rear, and had taken up a position near Bustee. A small force, consisting of 200 Gorkhas and 50 of the 4th Madras Cavalry, under Captain Clarke, had attacked and beaten 400 of them; but it was discovered that this was only the advanced guard, and that a much larger force was coming down upon the town. In this skirmish the detachment of Gorkhas formed line and advanced boldly, but after a few shots were fired, their line was resembled by an eye-witness to a " flock of geese," that is, " end on." The Madrasses here, under Captain Clarke, behaved gallantly, charging the enemy and disposing of thirty or forty, including their leader, one of the numerous family of " Sing," who are as well known as the Smiths of London. Captain Clarke then thought it necessary to retire from Bustee to Kuptangunge; but upon the force under Brigadier Rowcroft marching upon that place the same day, he was ordered to return and reoccupy the town.

The rebels seemed now to have completely surrounded us. Three or four thousand were still at Belwa in front; another column in our rear; 3000 or 4000 at Tandah, on the opposite side of the Gogra, on our left flank, threatening a move to our rear; while another body were not many miles from the town of Goruckpore. Under these circumstances it was thought advisable to retire that night with all speed to attack and disperse those near Bustee. At nine o'clock that night the camp was struck, the baggage was packed and sent off under a guard, while a number of Cooleys or Bildars were employed for three hours pulling down the walls and bastions of the small fort which had been constructed for the sick and baggage. The fort being pretty well defaced, the remainder of the force had cleared off the ground by ten o'clock that night.

The roads were very bad, and the difficulty of procuring sufficient conveyance for commissariat stores was so great that we did not arrive at Kuptangunge (twelve miles distant) until seven o'clock next morning. It was a most wearisome march, rendered particularly so by the sultriness of the night and the constant delays occasioned by the baggage. Either the hackeries must have been loaded more than usual, or the bullocks conspired not to work when urgently required. Sometimes they would rush frantically out of their frail yokes and scamper facetiously into a neighbouring field or village, giving a run to some unhappy driver. As luck would have it, the moon shed her benign rays on us, enlivening the scene a little, and after a space of nine hours, a march of twelve miles was performed. On one or two occasions, where more than ordinary obstinacy of the draft-bullocks caused a delay, a few managed to steal a sleep on the road-side, spreading a rug or greatcoat and laying their heads on a lump of dry mud for a pillow.

A Saes,* with a very valuable charger belonging to Major Richardson, went too far beyond the camping ground in company with his other servants and baggage. A party of the rebels being on the road at the time, captured him, to the great inconvenience of the owner, who lost at the same time all his clothes, letters, papers, and books. The Saes and another servant were murdered, but the rest escaped. Others had a narrow escape that same night, by getting in advance of the advanced guard, and going too far from the column. After this surprise the camp-followers entertained a wholesome fear of going too far from the tents.

About 1000 rebels were found to be in possession of the fort of Nuggur, seven miles

---

* A groom.

distant from our encampment, and another larger force, with artillery, was expected daily to join them from the other side of the river. On the 29th a detachment,* under the command of Major Cox, left the camp a little after noon, and having made a march of seven miles, took the enemy by surprise at half-past two o'clock, P.M. Approaching the jungle, which extends for a mile before reaching the village of Nuggur, and the old fort, which was surrounded by a high embankment and dry ditch, by the command of Major Cox the force made a detour, keeping the jungle half a mile to the right.

On getting within 500 yards of the village, the detachment was received with a heavy fire of musketry from the jungle and from behind the earthworks. Skirmishers of the

---

* 156 officers and men of Her Majesty's Light Infantry, 96 of the Naval Brigade, with two guns and a 24-pounder rocket-tube, 65 of the Bengal Yeomanry Cavalry, 202 Gorkhas, and 47 Sikhs.

13th Light Infantry, the Sikhs, and Royal Marines, were sent in to drive them out from their hiding-place, and from the rifle-pits with which it was intersected. The two naval guns and rocket under Lieutenant Grant, R.N., were ordered to take up a position on a slight rise and open fire on that part of the village where the enemy seemed to be most numerous. Here they were well peppered with shell; and the 24-pounder rockets pitching into the village, set it on fire, and, as well as the guns, aided to silence the musketry of the enemy. The Royal Marine and seamen skirmishers on the right, under Lieutenant Pym, Royal Marine Light Infantry, and a detachment of the 13th Light Infantry, under Captain Kerr, on the left, by a simultaneous movement, rushed into the village, and drove out the rebels, who made their escape through the jungle and across a Jheel which bordered the village. They formed upon the opposite side; but, owing to the nature of the ground, it was impossible for the cavalry to charge; consequently they effected their escape, leaving behind their baggage, tents, oxen, ponies, and large stores of grain, all of which was saved that escaped the conflagration. A sergeant of the 13th, collecting about a dozen men, pursued the enemy, and one of them, along with a Sikh, succeeded in capturing the rebels' colours as they escaped, disposing of the man who carried them with his rifle. Major Richardson's horse, which had been taken off a few days before, was now recaptured. His baggage, uniform, also books and clothes, which had been lost, were now found scattered in various places; no doubt distributed and subdivided by the captors. A man, who probably was on the point of walking off with the prize, was found killed by the bursting of a shell near the horse, so that he had a narrow escape from both causes. Thirty or forty of the rebels were killed, but the chief portion of them escaped; of our men only three or four were wounded. A kitmutgar of one of the officers was attacked by a budmash; but, although unarmed, he had more "pluck" than his opponent, and managing to deprive him of his tulwar, tied his hands behind his back, and triumphantly delivered him up to the magistrate.

Owing to the admirable arrangements that were made by Major Cox, the bold advance and sudden rush into the fort and village, the action was brought to a speedy and successful issue, with but a very trifling loss; and in the evening the detachment returned to camp, many of those who went out in the morning infantry having returned cavalry, being mounted on the ponies which were captured from the insurgents.

On crossing the Jheel, the rebels retreated with the utmost speed in the direction of Tandah, to join the other column which had been daily expected to make an inroad into the district. This sudden check, however, relieved it from any immediate prospect of such an incubus. And, further, it may be observed, that the field force left Amorha in the nick of time to save Bustee, and perhaps Goruckpore, from a second inundation.

CHAPTER X.

The Nepalese Army on its return Home—Government Servants mutilated—The Men lodged in Huts—A Locomotive Library—Recreation for the Men—Alarms—The First of the Dours—Attack on the Ranee's House at Amorha—The Rebels beaten at Hurreah.

BY this time Jung Bahadoor's army was at Fyzabad, *en route* for Nepaul, where there was some little delay, owing to the rebels at Belwa occupying the left bank of the river. By them they soon ceased to be molested: some said that there was a private understanding on the subject. For this I cannot positively vouch; at any rate, they crossed the Gogra without meeting with any opposition, and on the 10th of May, with unwonted celerity, the advanced guard surprised us by marching into Bustee. The whole force shortly after arrived, bringing in their train an amount of baggage borne on elephants, camels, hackeries, and ponies, one-tenth of which no one ever believed came from Nepaul; in fact, they returned rich in the spoils of Lucknow. No doubt they had much which would be regarded by Europeans as lumber; but in their estimation would be articles of value, and perhaps articles of *virtu*. The remaining Gorkha regiments, which had been with us so long, were now ordered home, and our force became diminished to about 730, out of which the number of the sick was alarming.

On the 7th of May the fort at Nuggur was destroyed, and on the following day the force marched to Bustee, which, being a central position, was made the head-quarters, and huts were ordered to be built for our men, instead of living in tents during the rains. A bungalow which had escaped the devastating genius of the Sepais, on their previous occupation of this village, was converted into a hospital, and in a very short time became crowded to excess. The climate now began to tell seriously on our men; almost all hands complained, more or less. The effects of living in a hothouse, with the thermometer ranging from 100° to 110°, varied with the unpleasantness of a dismal dust-storm, which obscured the light of the sun himself, was enough to make any one feel something more than "*ennui*," and cast a shadow of dulness over the force. Even the nights became so oppressive, that to expect relief even then was a vain hope. Day after day some one was cut off in the strength of his days, in a strange land, far from home, and without a relative to close his eyes. One day it was an officer, another day a non-commissioned officer, and sometimes a private; there was neither immunity nor precedence given to rank or age, when the cold hand of the last enemy clutched with an iron grasp.

Occasionally a dead or mutilated Tusseeldar, or other government officer, would appear in camp, upon whom a party of rebels made a dash, marching an amazing distance, and escaping again in one night. It was a brutalizing war, in which quarter was neither given or received. No European that fell into their hands could expect anything but a most cruel death, aggravated with great indignities, and therefore prisoners were not taken; for, if taken, it would only be to suffer execution in another form. Even to their own countrymen in the employment of government, they showed no mercy, sometimes even increasing in boldness and daring, making a fell swoop, from a distance, on some Theseel, or village, not many miles from our camp, and escaping before tidings could be conveyed of their approach.

By the middle of June the huts were finished, and on the 13th instant the Naval Brigade shifted billet into them from their tents. This was a great change for the better. The quarters were lofty and airy, the roof was made of straw, and sufficiently thick to repel the sun's rays, as well as to keep out the rain. Puncas were rigged up, and pulled all day by native punca wallas; added to which, the rains setting in, cooled the air, enabling the men to breathe. The sick list then began to fluctuate, and at last showed a diminution.

The season now became quite changed; an occasional thunderstorm was quite a variety, not an agreeable one, it must be acknowledged, to those who had the misfortune to be in tents, and were obliged to paddle in water; but when well housed, the country presented a different appearance, and the climate was by no means so oppressive as when the soil was parched and dry. The camp routine was as dull as usual. The drills were relaxed, the season not being suitable for that exercise, and all hands relapsed into reading or sleeping on a charpoy; a state which lasted for a longer or shorter period according to the state of the weather. No orders having arrived that the brigade should return to the ship, all hands settled down with the prospect of another campaign, and several kinds of amusements were got up for the men. Books were sent for, a reading-room was established, which, afterwards, when the force took the field, became a portable library, for which a tent was especially set apart. No sooner was the camp pitched after a march, than the reading-room tent, with the periodicals and daily papers, might be seen holding a conspicuous place. During the intervals of fine weather, divers athletic sports were got up for the men; jumping, racing, throwing shot for prizes, hurdle-racing, leaping and hopping. Sometimes it would be varied by a pony race, a Dhooley* race, or an Ecka

---

* A kind of palanquin for the sick or wounded, carried on men's shoulders.

race,* and occasionally the amusements of the day would be finished off as a great treat by an elephant race, or interrupted by a race between two or three Jacks dressed up in the costume of ladies of the last century, riding on donkeys with their feet touching the ground; and sometimes the grand finale would be a scamper, with loud shouts and vociferous cheering, after an unfortunate pig with his tail shaved.

In addition to these diurnal recreations there were theatricals in camp in the evening, or an occasional alarm in the night to keep up the excitement. There were bodies of insurgents constantly on the move, tossed about between one force and another, not knowing where to go, having much more reason to fear than to be feared; however, not knowing what desperate thing they might be tempted to do, it was always

---

* A small cart drawn by a pony. It is the Jarvey of India.

necessary to be on the " qui vive " whenever they were expected in the neighbourhood. At this time tawny wolves from the adjacent jungles paid periodical visits to the camp, and one fine night, when some of the camp-followers were up later than usual, cooking their supper, some of these hungry visitors considered they had a better right to the meal than the cooks, and coming unpleasantly close, the strangers scared the servants, who ran screaming, and causing such an alarm throughout the camp, that the sentries turned out the guard, and in less than ten minutes the brigade was under arms, and the guns were manned ready for action. On discovering their mistake, the men returned to their tents to have their legitimate residue of rest.

Not more than a fortnight afterwards, a jackal began to play his tricks, producing a still more alarming disturbance. He entered one of the men's huts late at night, and commenced a voyage of discovery among the mess-traps in quest of provender; he was driven away again and again, but not being offended at the repulse, exhibited a manifest reluctance to take his departure. He caught a pet monkey by the head, intending to make a meal off him in lieu of a better dish; but the pet was rescued, and the jackal ignominiously expelled from the hut. But not being bashful, he returned in a couple of hours, and began to make free with the limbs of one of the inmates of the hut, which caused the recipient of his attentions to leap out of bed and shout vociferously. Another messmate caught the infection, and jumped up half-asleep and half-awake, and, without having a very clear notion why, he laid hold of his neighbour violently, and both exerted their lungs to the utmost pitch. The other inmates of the tent were soon aroused by the noise, and an attempt was made to kill the invader, who managed in the confusion to make his escape. The men in the other huts were awakened from their peaceful slumbers by the "row," and ran out to discover what it was all about. A sentry seeing the men rushing from their huts, fired his musket; another sentry followed his example, giving the alarm; and in an incredibly short space of time the whole force was on the alert. The cavalry patrols came in at a gallop to see what was the matter, and more than one distinguished officer was seen emerging from his quarters in his shirt sleeves, with his sword in one hand and a revolver in the other; while some faithful bearer might be seen running with similar weapons of defence after his waking Sahib. In less than ten minutes there were men running in every direction to "see what was up;" while the jackal, no doubt, leisurely walked away, to wait for a more convenient opportunity to loot his dinner when the alarm had subsided.

After the taking of Lucknow, when flying columns had been sent after the rebels by the Commander-in-Chief, traversing Oudh in different directions, they became split up into many detached forces, and when driven from one place would reappear a few days afterwards in another; until at last they took refuge on the north side of the Gogra, having much fewer troops there to molest them than in Oudh. With the increase of 300 of the 6th Madras Cavalry, under Colonel Byng, the Goruckpore field force at Bustee amounted to about 1000 men. Even with so small a force it was necessary so to dispose them that the insurgents should get no rest; but being hunted down wherever they appeared, should never be permitted to take root in any particular locality. For this purpose the force was split up into small detachments, and sent to scour all parts of the district. This was anything but a pleasant duty during the rains. When a dour of this kind was made, the dry hut and comfortable quarters were left behind at Bustee, and at the end of a long and wearisome march, the tents would be pitched where the ground was wet under foot, and with rain falling over head, the whole country was either a sheet of water or a muddy marsh, adding the appearance of dreariness to the experience of discomfort.

The first of these dours was commenced on the 23rd of May, when a detachment of two guns, and a 24-pounder rocket-tube of the Naval Artillery, with two troops of the Bengal Yeomanry Cavalry, marched to Kuptangunge to hold it as an outpost; and after a halt of a few days proceeded to Hurreah. On the 31st of the same month, one of these wandering bodies of rebels attacked, looted, and burned the village of Kuptangunge. The Theseeldar and inhabitants fled to Bustee with all speed to give the alarm; but before assistance could be rendered all the mischief was done, and they were off.

On the 7th of June another detachment, consisting of twenty of the Royal Marine Light Infantry, and thirty-two of H.M.'s 13th Light Infantry, under Lieutenant Pym, Royal Marine Light Infantry, marched from Bustee at nine o'clock at night, and by three o'clock next morning arrived at Kuptangunge, where other troops were drawn up on the road ready to march. They then proceeded to Hurreah, where another small detachment had just arrived under Major Cox, who had left Bustee on the 30th of May, and after taking a circuitous route, and scouring the district in another direction, arrived here in time to take the command. The tents were pitched, and the troops, some of whom had completed a twenty-two miles march, lay down to rest for a few hours, until six o'clock the same day, when the tents were struck, and the baggage packed. At two o'clock next morning, they* marched in the direction of Amorha in two columns, one under the command of Major Richardson, consisting of a detachment of Royal Marines, 13th Light Infantry, and a few Sikhs, with one troop of cavalry and two guns. While this column proceeded along the road, the other, led by Major Cox, went across country to attack the enemy, strongly posted in the house of a Ranee near Amorha. At daylight the force arrived at a nullah in the rear of the house and village, from behind which the rebels opened fire on the cavalry. The Royal Marines coming up, were thrown out in skirmishing order, and returned the fire; the guns, under Lieutenant Turnour, R.N., were galloped up, and threw shot and

---

* "Pearl's" Naval Brigade, 53; two 12-pounder howitzers, and one 24-pounder rocket-tube; 200 of the 13th Light Infantry; two troops of the 6th Madras Cavalry, two troops of the Bengal Yeomanry Cavalry, and 20 Sikhs.

shell among the main body, which after a quarter of an hour retreated into the house and adjacent buildings. The force then forded the nullah, and throwing out skirmishers, Major Cox, with his usual skill and bravery, forced them to evacuate their position, and drove them towards Belwa. Several were killed in the retreat; our loss was inconsiderable. After a short halt, the force returned to Hurreah, and bildars were employed to destroy the fort which they had rebuilt at Amorha. The Royal Marines continued their march to Bustee, an attack being expected there from another quarter.

It is painful to be obliged to call to mind that the graves of those who fell in action, or died from disease, during the time we were encamped at Amorha, were torn open by the rebels after we left it; such was their savage barbarity, that even the bones of the dead were not allowed to rest in peace. The graves were then restored, and the damage was rectified before leaving the place. On the return of the force to Bustee, the rebels came on again with imperturbable pertinacity, and returning to Hurreah, seemed disposed to take up their quarters there during the rains, commencing to throw up earthworks and build huts. But on the 16th of June, another dour was made in the same direction. At seven o'clock in the evening, eighty seamen and marines under Captain Sotheby, one troop of Bengal Yeomanry Cavalry, and half a troop of Madras Cavalry, left Bustee, and by half past ten at night, arriving near Kuptangunge, they lay down on the road to rest until daybreak, intending to take the enemy by surprise at Hurreah. But as they were about to push on, a fearful thunder-storm broke over their heads; rain fell in torrents; no tents were pitched to give shelter, the land was flooded, the road was turned into a river, and all hands were well drenched. A dram of rum was issued to the men, and they managed to get as far as the camping ground. The land being a sheet of water, was not in a very good condition for the working of guns. The attack was consequently postponed until the following day (the 18th), when, at three o'clock in the morning, having joined another detachment which had been sent out previously under Lieutenant-Colonel Byng of the 6th Madras Cavalry, the force* left Kuptangunge to attack the insurgents under Mahomed Hussein, who were posted and entrenched in the village of Hurreah, eight miles in front. At midnight 150 of the Bengal Yeomanry Cavalry

* "Pearl's" Naval Brigade, 111; two 12-pounder howitzers, and one 24-pounder rocket-tube, under Captain Sotheby; 135 of the 13th Light Infantry; 50 Sikhs; 130 Bengal Yeomanry Cavalry; 100 of the 6th Madras Cavalry; one 9-pounder and one 24-pounder howitzer, Bengal Artillery.

and 6th Madras Cavalry, under the command of Captain Mulcaster, went across country by a circuitous route, and after a fatiguing march of sixteen miles, took up a position in the rear of the enemy, masked by a tope of trees, with a view of cutting off their retreat, and if possible capture their chief, with his guns and elephants. About three o'clock in the morning of the 18th, the remainder of the force marched to meet the enemy in front.

The Nazim Mahomed Hussein had taken up a position with about 4000 or 5000 men, including 900 Sepais and six guns, in the villages of Sirsaie and Hurreah. On the right flank were two thick bamboo jungles and a village in the possession of the enemy, and on the left flank a nullah, a village, and a strong brick house, besides a tope of trees also occupied by them.

Captain Mulcaster and Captain Chapman continued to watch the enemy's movements until a little after sunrise, when the action commenced. Skirmishers were thrown out, and the guns were brought up to the front and opened fire. The enemy stood firm until the troops began to close; then, under the influence of the artillery and the steady advance of the riflemen driving them across the river, which, the skirmishers of the 13th, under Lieutenant Everett, the Royal Marines and seamen under Mr. Ingles, mate, immediately fording, they retired from the bridge. Captain Sotheby galloped up the naval guns, and finding the right in close collision with the enemy's left, who obstinately held the jungle, opened a destructive fire with shot and shell. All this time the cavalry were exposed to a continued and heavy fire from the enemy's rifles and infantry, who were in a position inaccessible to cavalry. Captain Chapman with his troop took a wide sweep, to cut off the elephants and baggage, which were at some distance; but being in a position inaccessible to cavalry, the movement had only the effect of causing some of it to be abandoned.

The two guns of the Bengal Artillery and the remainder of the 13th having been, with Lieutenant-Colonel Byng, engaged on the left, now advanced, took up a position on the road, and shelled the rebels out of the jungle; and the two naval guns, galloping over the bridge, found the enemy in great force. On the right, at a distance of 300 yards, a small mud battery was thrown up, with well-made embrasures, in order to command the bridge, and another in a tope about double the distance off. From the former they were soon cleared out by the howitzers; and as they were retreating from the latter, where they appeared to be a strong column of 1500 men, their movements were accelerated by the same agency. The naval guns here coming up with the skirmishers and the Bengal Yeomanry Cavalry at the same time, they were pursued until the infantry, from fatigue and intolerable heat, were obliged to halt.

The enemy, who were evidently trained soldiers, retired in good order, receiving protection from the numerous topes and small villages on their route. The action lasted four hours, and they are reported to have lost about seventy. Our casualty list was small, only seven or eight men, and several horses wounded. The naval guns under Lieutenant Turnour, assisted by Mr. Maquay, mate, R.N., were remarked to have moved with great rapidity, and to have fired with great precision. There was only one of the enemy's captured, with some of their baggage and ammunition. That part of the district was, however, cleared for the present, and the Nazim effected his escape, and that but narrowly; he was obliged to retire into the jungle, there to take up his quarters in an old fort, with a few trusty followers.

The force did not long remain at Hurreah, and two days afterwards had the benefit of another thunder-storm, which caused the men in tents to be "all afloat;" a circumstance by no means conducive to the well-being of the troops, or calculated to restore to health those who had lately been suffering from fever or dysentery. But these inconveniences never produced discontent whenever there was active service to be carried out; let the weather be ever so trying, or the heat ever so oppressive, the men were at all times ready, forward, and even impatient to leave the sick list before the time.

CHAPTER XI.

Engagement with the Rebels near Lumptee—Attack on Hurreah—The Rebels beaten at Debreah—Dour to Bansee—Harassing March—The Rebels Beaten at Doomureahgunge—Second Dour to Bansee—The Enemy beaten at Amorha—Jugdespore attacked—Rebels routed at Doomureahgunge—Rebels attacked at Bururiah.

On the 29th of August a detachment of the Naval Brigade under Lieutenant Fawkes, R.N., took part in an action near Lumptee. The force,* under the command of Captain Garrard of the 27th Regiment, Native Infantry, repelled, with unshaken steadiness and promptitude, an attack of the enemy under the Rajah of Gondah, consisting of 150

---

* "Pearl's" Naval Brigade, 50, with two guns; 50 of Her Majesty's 13th Light Infantry; 50 Sikhs; 350 of the 27th Madras Native Infantry; one troop of the 6th Madras Cavalry.

Sowars, 300 Sepais, and 1900 irregular troops, with four guns. By the time the enemy's advanced guard got within two miles of the entrenchments, the detachment of Her Majesty's 13th Light Infantry was ordered to take up a position on the left of the road in a tope, and the detachment of the 27th Madras Native Infantry on the right, under cover of a village. The seamen and guns took ground in the centre, in another village. The enemy advanced in three columns, and attacked the left and centre several times, but were repelled by the steady firing of the rifles and the effective precision of the shells. The attack was kept up until about four o'clock, P.M., when they attempted to turn the flank of the position taken up by Captain Garrard; but failing in this, they retired, and the force followed them up, the guns and cavalry pursuing, until they halted and recommenced the firing. The naval guns then advanced rapidly, and silenced their battery, forcing them to retreat. After a pursuit of three or four miles, the force returned to Amorha. The loss of the enemy was about fifty; our detachment suffered very slightly.

On the same day, about half-past five in the evening, another attack was made by the rebels on another outpost at Hurreah, eight miles distant. They were about 800 strong, with a force in reserve, and three guns. Intelligence of the fact was immediately sent to headquarters at Bustee, and at ten o'clock that night a force* was sent out with the utmost rapidity under Major Cox, of the 13th Light Infantry. They had been repelled by Captain Vine with his small detachment; but on the approach of the reinforcement from Bustee, and on the arrival of the cavalry in advance at two o'clock next morning, they lost no time in retiring.

Major Cox immediately pushed on to

---

* 350 of Her Majesty's 13th Light Infantry; two guns of Naval Brigade under Lieutenant Turnour; one troop of Bengal Yeomanry Cavalry.

Debreah, where he again came up with them on the 1st of September. They numbered about 1000 infantry, fifty Sowars, and three guns. After a fatiguing march, he attacked, defeated, and routed them, Major Cox himself leading a party of the 13th to a charge against a body of the rebels concealed behind the embankment of a tank, clearing them out, and with the whole detachment pursued them up close, until they retired with a loss of about ninety in killed and wounded; the detachment at the same time suffering much from bad roads, oppressive heat, and heavy ground; but they went through it with their usual cheerfulness and steadiness, inspired by the intrepidity of their leader with a confidence of success.

On the evening of the 6th of September another dour was made by a detachment under the command of Commander Grant, R.N., at a season of the year most trying to the strongest constitution and most undaunted perseverance; but was conducted with a zeal and judgment which deservedly gained the highest commendation from the Brigadier in command. The force consisted of two 12-pounder howitzers, and a 24-pounder rocket-tube, with seventy-three seamen and marines, and seventy non-commissioned officers, rank and file, of Her Majesty's 13th Light Infantry, under Lieutenant Gillett. The object was to relieve Bansee, a town in the northern part of the district of Goruckpore, which belonged to a friendly Rajah; the small garrison of Sikhs who held the place, being hard pressed by the rebels, a prompt and speedy march of a sufficient force was the only chance for its safety.

On reaching Gontah, twelve miles distant from the place, Captain Mulcaster joined the detachment with a squadron of cavalry, and assuming the command, pushed on with all speed, and arrived at Bansee on the 8th, after a march of fifty miles, in thirty-nine hours.

The roads were in a deplorable state after the rains. The guns were carried on elephants. The men were sometimes marching up to their knees in mud, and sometimes up to their waist in water, Jack suggesting that a boat would be more suitable. In one place they waded for nearly three miles, besides having forded two nullahs and crossed another in a boat, which with some difficulty was procured for the purpose. In addition to the difficulties under foot, the sun, as usual, poured down his rays of fire, which was most harassing to the men, who, nevertheless, pushed on, and the enemy, on hearing of their approach, retired. Then the Raptee, a river deep and rapid at that season of the year, was crossed by a portion of the force, and the cavalry pursuing the fugitives cut up several.

Havildar Narain Sing, of the Sikh battalion, leaving his corps, galloped on, and having cut down two of the enemy, returned to his men; and on a subsequent occasion this same native Sikh officer, on the retreat of the enemy across a river, threw off his clothes, and taking his sword between his teeth, swam across and cut down five of the rebels.

On arriving at the house of the Rajah, which was converted into a sort of fortress, it was found that the ammunition of the Sikh garrison had run so short, that only three rounds of percussion-caps remained per man. Here the Europeans got shelter from the sun; but having out-marched the commissariat, were without provisions until nine o'clock at night. The Sikhs, to stay the cravings of hunger, commenced to make chupatties (a sort of thin native cake baked in a pan), which were very acceptable under the circumstances; but Jack gave it as his opinion that they had the flavour of baked sawdust

Brigadier Fischer, of the Madras Native Infantry, joined the force on the 10th, and on the 12th marched from Bansee, a few men having been left behind who were thoroughly "done up" with fatigue, heat, and exposure. The rest of the force, losing no time, reached Doomureahgunge on the 13th, when the advanced guard was fired upon by a body of rebels from a line of earthworks commanding the road. The naval guns (12-p^r mountain-train howitzers) having been taken off the backs of the elephants, and the horses being yoked to them, were speedily galloped to the front; the marines and seamen, under Lieutenant Ingles, advanced at the double to cover their guns. The infantry forming line advanced steadily to the front, waded over fields flooded with water, and on coming within range, the guns opened fire, throwing shell into their entrenched camp and on the main body, until they were obliged to retire.

Next day, with indomitable perseverance, the force crossed the river, and marched northward towards Intwa, expecting to catch the enemy in a village where they had taken up their quarters; but the roads being quite impassable without swimming, they were obliged to return and recross the river. The object of the expedition being accomplished, they marched back to Bustee, which was reached on the 17th; and the following morning the sick, who were left behind, also arrived at head-quarters.

A similar expedition, if possible, more harassing, was subsequently made by another detachment[*] of the Naval Brigade under Lieutenant Ingles, which left Bustee on the 27th of the same month, and arriving at Bansee by forced marches, crossed the

---

[*] "Pearl's" Naval Brigade, two 12-pounder howitzers, 30 men and 2 officers, under Lieutenant Ingles, R.N.; 72 of Her Majesty's 13th Light Infantry, under Colonel Twynan, and 27 of the Bengal Yeomanry Cavalry.

Raptee and came up with the rear-guard of the rebels at Mowee. The cavalry and guns quickly dispersed them, driving them into the jungle; and after a pursuit of five or six miles, the force returned, having suffered greatly from a hard day's work, wading through water, and scouring through thick jungle.

The rebels, driven from Oudh, were daily increasing on the north of the Gogra, and the Goruckpore field force was obliged to do the work of double their number. It was split up into small detachments, which were continually despatched to drive off wandering bands of insurgents, who were becoming more and more audacious in their approaches, from having no spot of ground which they could calculate on as a safe retreat. Sometimes they would make a dash at some village, mutilating or killing the Theseeldar or some unfortunate Burkundazee, and then looting the neighbourhood, would make their escape. The movements of these flying columns were so rapid, that it was quite impossible to get timely intelligence of their approach, and equally impossible to calculate where they intended to go, or what turning they were next likely to take. One of these wandering clouds passed within ten miles of Bustee, and killed two Madras Saeses (grooms) which they met on the road. Captain Sotheby, in company with Commander Turnour, had a narrow escape, having ridden along the road only half an hour before they crossed. The same day the Naval Brigade was in danger of suffering a severe loss in its commanding officer from another cause. He was much injured by a bad fall from his horse, but fortunately the injury turned out not to be so severe as was anticipated, and after a temporary indisposition, Captain Sotheby was again restored to duty. Such are the many chances that flutter about in time of war.

While the proceedings just narrated were carrying out in the north of the district, another affair took place in the west of it towards Fyzabad. The detachment which held the outpost at Amorha, was attacked on October 1st about noon. The villagers reported that the enemy, numbering about 1200, with two guns, were advancing in three columns, their usual order, one on the centre, and one on each flank. Captain Garrard, of the 27th Native Infantry, was in command. The detachment* moved out, and took up a position at a distance of about 800 yards in front of the camp. The seamen and Sikhs took ground in the centre, and a small body of Infantry were thrown out on both flanks.

About two o'clock in the afternoon, the

---

* Fifty of the "Pearl's" Naval Brigade and two 12-pounder howitzers under Lieutenant Fawkes; 50 of the 13th Light Infantry; 50 Sikhs; 70 Madras Infantry, and one troop of Madras Cavalry.

enemy commenced the attack on both flanks and centre, which was renewed several times; but being repulsed each time by the rifles and shell, towards evening they commenced a retreat, when they were hotly pursued by the horsed guns, supported by the cavalry and Sikhs. The cavalry charging on the left, and the guns directed by Lieutenant Maquay, pursuing them with unexpected speed, came within a short distance of several of the retreating mutineers. A few of the cavalry advanced, intending to charge, but on approaching too near, the Sepais went through threatening motions with their muskets, causing either the horses or their riders to turn about. An attempt was made more than once to bring them to the point, but the Sepais kept them at bay. Four of the seamen at the gun were ordered to charge; an order which they gallantly obeyed. Lee, Williams, Rayfield, and Simmonds, dashed forward, and came up with a few that still had not made their escape; after a short encounter, the clash of swords being but for a moment, and they were despatched. Lee received a severe sword-cut in the arm, Rayfield a slight contusion in the arm, which was said to have been a bite from the Sepai when deprived of his other weapon, and Williams only a very slight wound. The affair being thus brought to a termination, the detachment returned to camp.

On the 23rd of October, another dour was made to Bansee, the rebels again coming down to that neighbourhood. The force consisted of a detachment of the Bengal Yeomanry Cavalry, two naval guns, and a company of H.M.'s 13th Light Infantry; and having had a brush with the enemy, returned to head-quarters. On the 26th of the same month, an attack was made by a detachment under the command of Colonel Lord Mark Kerr, 13th Light Infantry, on

Jugdespore, a fort in the jungle, lying about twenty-five miles north-west from Bustee, which being more strongly garrisoned than had been expected, his lordship drew off his men in good order, and retired. This movement gave rise to reports that the Naval Brigade guns were taken; and many amusing letters on the subject were written in the Indian papers by the seamen, in which they indignantly repelled the charge, expressing their astonishment that the public were ignorant of the fact that there are two things Jack never loses, and these are "his grog and his guns."

The outlying detachments having been called in, the whole field force marched from Bustee, on the 24th of November, towards the north of the district. The rebels by this time having been routed out of Oudh and the Dooab, congregated along the belt of jungle which separates our territory from Nepaul. A field hospital was established at Bustee, and small detachments from the different corps left as a guard, Lieutenant-Colonel Whistler, of the 6th Madras Cavalry, being in command. A siege train also arriving at Bustee, the same day, was ordered to join the force, and subsequently was turned over to the " Pearl's" Naval Brigade.

On the 25th the force marched to Bhanpore, and was there joined by a Madras battery, under the command of Captain Cadell, and next day moved on to Doomureahgunge, which is situated on the right bank of the Raptee. When within two miles of the village, a native brought information that our bugle-calls on the line of march were heard by the advanced piquet of the rebels, and that they were preparing to retreat. The brigade soon after halted, on the enemy being seen on the left, not more than a mile distant. Sowars were observed riding up and down, in front of the infantry, which had taken up a position in a mango-tope. A detachment was sent out under Lieutenant-Colonel Cox, of the 13th Light Infantry, consisting of 200 Sikhs of the Ferozepore regiment, under Lieutenant-Colonel Brazier, 200 of the 13th Light Infantry, and two guns of Captain Cadell's battery, with a troop of cavalry. While Colonel Cox attacked the insurgents on the left of the road, the remainder of the force, under Brigadier Rowcroft, consisting of the rest of the 13th, the Sikhs, the Naval Brigade and Artillery, advanced along the road towards the village, in order to cut off any possibility of escape in that direction. As soon as the Madras Artillery got within range, Captain Cadell opened fire with his guns, and soon drove them out of the tope. The detachment still pressed on, driving them before them as they went, until they "shoved" them up into the bend of a nullah, out of which they could not extricate themselves without either fighting or swimming; the latter course they preferred.

The cavalry charged down the bank of the nullah, and drove them into the water; not, however, without the loss of their brave leader, Captain Gifford, and a trooper, who were killed, and several others wounded. A scene then was acted which could not be witnessed in a warfare between two civilized European nations. The war in India was a war of extermination, without any shadow of doubt; the crime not only of the Sepais who mutinied and killed their officers, but of the other rebels, who, unprovoked, took a savage delight in the blood of Europeans, was such that the universal feeling which prevailed was " death" to the perpetrators. It was utterly impossible to discover the men among the multitudes who had done the deeds, and therefore all who bore arms against the Government were regarded as being implicated. In this state of things few ever went through the empty formality of making prisoners.

Many of the Sepais who escaped the sabres of the cavalry, were drowned in the nullah, when making an attempt to escape; and many others appeared with only their black heads above water, making the last vain effort to save life, either by wading or swimming. It is only when there is no chance of escape that the natives of India exhibit great courage, or rather indifference, at meeting death. When an opportunity offers to get away, they show no greater contempt for life than other people. The heads of the fugitives dotted about then became marks to fire at, until all disappeared, except one or two, who, escaping among a shower of balls, crawled up the opposite bank, and hid among the high crops. One, in particular, was standing up to his chin in the water, unable to swim across, and submitting to the annoyance of being the object of many "pot shots," for nearly half an hour. An officer's servant, his fellow countryman, showing his zeal for the "Company Bahadoor," commenced firing missiles, in the form of lumps of hard clay, which were the first to take effect. An officer standing by charged him with the folly of being a rebel, and told him that he was going that day to receive the reward of his deeds in the other world; stating it in plainer language than I have thought it necessary to write. He replied with a volley of abuse, in no measured or choice language, and told him it was no business of his. A torrent of foul epithets ensued: but in this kind of warfare it is hopeless for a European to compete with a native of India. Their language abounds in such a choice collection of insulting terms, that it is incomparably rich in untranslateable slang. In fact I have heard of men in the bazaars who would not object to attack any one with lingo for a very small remuneration. Whether this individual was a member of that profession or not, it was impossible to ascertain; at any rate his time was drawing to a close, for a trooper then coming up, fired, and the wretched man made one struggle—for a moment the water was disturbed—but the next minute and the circling ripples subsided; he sunk to rise no more, and all was as calm above as if nothing had happened.

One small gun and limber was taken, and the force retired. But on halting for a short time to rest the troops, an officer going into a field of dhall, was saluted by a Sepai in full uniform, with a Punjab medal on his breast, who presented his musket, but did not fire. Being only armed with a sword, he called a soldier of the 13th, who despatched him, and as he retired, boasting how well he had done it, a more experienced campaigner immediately proceeded to denude him of the medal, and investigate the contents of his kamerband, in which was discovered a large deposit of Company's rupees. It was considered scarcely equitable that another should step in and capture the proceeds of his prize. To rifle the slain for the gold mohurs or Company's rupees, became of such usual occurrence, the Sepais carrying their property in their kamerband, or turban, that the man who made the "bag" (a sporting expression in common use) had a vested interest in his antagonist.

There was a halt at Doomureahgunge for some days, while a bridge of boats was constructing across the Raptee. Balla Rao, a brother, as some call him, or some other near relative of the Nana, as others say, occupied the opposite side with several thousand men and a strong force of artillery. He continued collecting revenue at the rate of about 5000 rupees per day, and report said that he sent his salaams to the Begum, offering her cash, and informing her of his successes. The former she is said to have declined, not being in any immediate want of subsidies, but as to the latter she congratulated him.

On the evening of the 2nd, Brigadier Rowcroft received intelligence that the force under the Nazim Mahomed Hossein, of about 2000 or 3000 men, with six guns, had left his fort at Bungaon, and with the utmost effrontery encamped only six or eight miles distant from our camp higher up the river, evidently with a view of crossing over and joining Balla Rao.

On the 3rd of December, a portion of the force under the command of Brigadier Rowcroft, went out to attack him. Two guns and fifty men of the Naval Brigade, under Captain Sotheby, C.B., 350 of

H.M.'s 13th Light Infantry, a detachment of Sikhs, the Bengal Yeomanry Cavalry, a detachment of the 27th Madras Native Infantry, with four guns of Captain Cadell's battery—about 850 men of all arms—went out about half-past five in the morning, and about eight o'clock found the enemy protected behind mud walls and earthworks, in the village of Bururiah, and in two large woods with a thick forest and jungle to retire to behind. There was some broken ground in front, a difficulty which was soon overcome. The enemy opened fire with three guns and musketry, when Captain Sotheby's two guns in the centre, and two of Captain Cadell's on the left, with two others in charge of Captain Highmoor on the right, quickly responded. The enemy at first stood their ground more firmly than usual, the naval guns and Madras battery playing upon them with round-shot, shell, and grape. They held to their trenches obstinately, until the steady and resistless advance shook their resolution. The seamen and marines went close up to their works in front in skirmishing order, under a heavy fire, while the Sikhs and a company of the 13th skirted the jungle to the left; the enemy then finding themselves threatened on the flank, relinquished their position and commenced a retreat. And being favoured by the woods and thick cover, they managed to get their guns over a small river where there was a ford, and into the forest, where they were driven after a two hours' combat, having been expelled from the woods and villages.

The rebel force becoming scattered, there were several parties who seemed to go " on their own hook" as they expressed it, and took a few "pot shots" at any stray Sowars who might be fluttering about. On any of them making their appearance, " crack," " crack," quickly followed, and his retreat was either hastened, or he fell. The loss of the enemy was reckoned to be between thirty and forty; two seamen were wounded, and of the other corps, there were about twelve wounded. The number of hair-breadth escapes were about the same as usual on these occasions, such as a bullet through some part of the clothes, or having a badge taken off a helmet, or some trifle of that sort. After a short halt, the force returned to camp, fatigued and hungry, at three o'clock in the afternoon.

CHAPTER XII.

The Rebels enclosed in a Net—The Force encamped at Intwa—Obedience of Elephants—The Force marches into Oudh—Battle of Toolseepore—The Siege Train—The Town of Toolseepore after the Battle.

ON the 5th of December, the bridge of boats was complete, and the Naval Brigade crossed to the north side of the river. The sick and wounded were sent to Bustee, to the field hospital, and now Brigadier Rowcroft's column was moving northward inclining to the west so as to enclose the shattered forces of the Begum, which were hemmed in on all sides in the northern district of Oudh. The Commander-in-Chief, Lord Clyde, was moving down upon them from the westward. Sir Hope Grant, with a large force of cavalry, was moving up from the south, and Brigadier Rowcroft's column was drawing round from the east, while the Nepaul jungles were on the north. Here the last grand smash was to take place of those marauding mutineers who had made many a home sad for the previous two years. And with this grand finale, the "Pearl's" Naval Brigade wound up their two campaigns in India. The arrangements were admirably made. The southern districts of Oudh had been cleared by the numerous flying columns which had traversed it in every direction, and they were all hunted up into this one corner of the country. The Queen's well-timed proclamation had been read, and many availed themselves of the royal clemency; but all those who could not convince themselves that any Government could be so merciful as to extend the golden sceptre of favour after all that had been perpetrated, or still clinging to the last hope in a failing cause, fled to the north, expecting, when unable to stand in the open field, to be able to take shelter in the jungles of Nepaul.

After crossing the river, the force marched to Intwa, leaving a detachment at Doomureahgunge to guard the bridge of boats and ghat. The camping ground was an open plain, where we halted for several days, and the siege train, which was handed over to the Naval Brigade, was here parked in front of our camp.

The field force now began to muster strong, consisting of the Ferozpore regiment of Sikhs, about 600 men; H.M.'s 13th Light Infantry, nearly an equal number; 300 of the 6th Madras Cavalry, a Madras battery, the Bengal Yeomanry Cavalry, and the Naval Brigade. The several corps were daily drilled in front of the lines, and the band played in the evening for the benefit of those who attended the promenade; the weather at this season is delightful, but it lasts only two or three months. The days are not unpleasantly warm, and the nights are cool, in fact sometimes they are biting cold; and on going outside the tents soon after sunrise a noble view of the snowy range of the Hymalayas can be seen lifting up to heaven their white crests tinted with a roseate hue, as they glitter in the beams of the rising sun. On the 18th the siege train arrived from Doomureahgunge—two 18-pounders, one 8-inch howitzer, and two 8-inch mortars; these, in addition to two $5\frac{1}{2}$-inch mortars, were turned over to the "Pearl's" Naval Brigade. Every seaman and marine was now attached to the siege train, with the exception of those who manned the light field battery of four 12-p^r howitzers and two 9-pounders. The men had become sufficiently acquainted with the management of horses, bullocks, and elephants to feel quite at home among them. One elephant became quite a pet among the men—rather a clumsy one, we must admit, becoming so tame that he paid a daily visit to the several tents to receive donations, in the form of bread, and on his arrival announced himself with the sniff of his proboscis, or a touch of a tent rope. The elephants that are used for beasts of burden are caught in the jungle, and soon become domesticated, but do not breed in a tame state. They are wonderful animals—so powerful, and yet so gentle, so clumsy, and apparently so void of intelligence, yet so docile; they are so capable of resisting, so violent and untameable when they become infuriated, perfectly regardless whom they tread down in their blind rage, and yet generally so obedient to command. When the mahout speaks, he seems to understand. When he tells him what to do, he obeys. Occasionally he is brought to the river to bathe; the mahout standing on his back drives him into the deep water, where he flounders about for some time, projecting the extremity of his trunk above the surface to breathe. He is then brought to the shallow water, where he lies down on one side, while he is rubbed and washed, and then is turned on the other for the same operation; all this time paying the utmost deference to the orders of the mahout. He rolls about like a huge monster, and after playing for some time and apparently enjoying the bath, returns to his "moorings," where he is attached to a tree by a chain round his hind leg.

Captain Sotheby had now got the command of a formidable armament, and it would have been difficult, if not impossible, to have procured artillerymen at so short a notice so well trained, or better fitted to manage heavy guns. The four mortars were in the charge of Lieutenant Pym, R.M., Light Infantry, and his detachment of Royal Marines, and Marine Artillery.

It was expected that the rebels would make a last dying struggle at the fortress of Toolseepore in the north of Oudh, and in order to finish off the campaign with as little delay as possible, these heavy guns were sent on with the force. Toolseepore was one of the last that held out when Oudh was annexed, and being of great strength it was impossible to say that its owner, who belonged to the insurgent party, might not resist to the last.

On the morning of the 20th, the force marched from Intwa to Biskohur on the Oudh frontier: the boundary line between Goruckpore and that kingdom being marked by small pillars two or three hundred yards apart, ran through our camp, so that some of the force were in Goruckpore and some in Oudh. The morning was as dismal as both tradition and experience combine to prove a December morning to be. The road was wretchedly bad, owing to heavy rains that usually fall at this season of the year; a thick mist enveloped everything, and through it the sun made sundry abortive efforts to shine. The cold, early in the morning, was intense, and the damp mist rendered it still more so. The horses sunk in the mud up to their knees, and many of the baggage-carts did not arrive on the camping ground until late that night; the bullocks being unable to drag them along with their wheels becoming embedded in the tenacious liquid mud. When the tents were pitched, rain threatened, and a small trench was dug round the frail tenement to catch the water, and a little embankment was thrown up all around to keep it out; and on the 22nd, the force marched to Goolereah Ghat, and encamped on the bank of the Boora Raptee, not more than five miles from Toolseepore, where the enemy were assembled in great force.

Brigadier Rowcroft had an interview with Sir Hope Grant the same day, from whom orders were received to attack the rebels on the following morning. The Brigadier suffered a severe loss this day in the departure of the 1st Punjab Cavalry, which went *en route* for the Commander-in-Chief's camp, and being on the eve of a battle, if their services had been secured for one day longer, the success would have been much more complete and satisfactory. They are a noble corps, well mounted, and a fine race of men; they go by the name of Hughes' Horse, and are an irregular regiment, a sort of yeomanry; the troopers belonging to a respectable class in their own country, supplying their own horses, and being paid a liberal monthly allowance. In lieu of them H.M.'s 53rd regiment was sent to join our forces, and arrived that night, and although a regiment of veterans than whom none could do their work better, a cavalry regiment was much more required at that time.

23rd of December.—Having had an early breakfast this morning, at half-past six o'clock the tents were struck, and the baggage was packed, so as to be ready to follow at the conclusion of the action. The force forded the river between nine and ten o'clock; the siege train from its cumbrousness occupying some time, but considering the steepness of the banks, and the nature of the soil, was transported with more speed than would have been anticipated. The large guns were drawn by elephants, and the mortars by twenty-four bullocks. When the whole force had crossed, the line was formed, and, under the orders of Brigadier Rowcroft, advanced towards the enemy, who were seen about two miles distant on an extensive open plain, with a few villages scattered here and there, which they turned to account by occupying them with a party of infantry and guns. They were, as usual, well aware how to make use of every available position, which was as expeditiously relinquished when hard pressed, as it was originally well chosen.

H.M.'s 13th Light Infantry, under the command of Lord Mark Kerr, took ground on the extreme right; on their left was the Madras battery of four guns, under Captain Cadell, and the Bengal Yeomanry Cavalry (200 sabres); on the extreme left of the line were a body of the 27th Madras Native Infantry, and between 200 and 300 of the 6th Madras Cavalry; next on their right was H.M.'s 53rd regiment, under Colonel English, and between the 53rd and the Ferozpore regiment of Sikhs, under Colonel Brazier, were the four naval guns and two 24-lb. rocket tubes under the command of Commander Turnour, R.N. Lieutenant Maquay and Mr. C. Foot, midshipman, being also attached to the battery. The Naval Brigade and siege train, under the command of Captain Sotheby, C.B., kept as close to the line as the nature of the ground, which was intersected with small watercourses, would admit.

All the men, both seamen and marines, were now turned into gunners; so that, with the exception of the four 12-p^r howitzers and rockets, there was little opportunity for the others to take part in the action; these, with which Captain Sotheby was ever present, pushed on to the front, and notwithstanding the rough character of the ground, were conspicuous for the rapidity of their movements, and the speed of their advance in close proximity to the skirmishers of the 53rd, as they pursued and routed the enemy. "Come on, boys," said some of the soldiers, and Jack limbered up, vowed he would go anywhere, and on he dashed, managing the horses and guns with such activity and readiness, that some of them said, using an expletive better suppressed, "Well, I'll believe anything about sailors after this."

On the right, the 13th attacked a village, where a large body of rebels with a gun had taken up a position under cover of the mud walls; as they advanced the enemy kept up a heavy fire of shot and musketry, but the soldiers entered it with a rush, took one gun at the point of the bayonet, and bayoneted the gunner who persisted in sticking to his idol* to the last. Another gunner was found with his brains blown out, apparently with his own hand, seeing no chance of escape. On the left, the 53rd, the Sikhs, the four naval guns, and the two 24-lb. rocket tubes, were pushed rapidly forward. The rebels here seem to have stood their ground much better than usual. They waited under cover of a bank of a nullah until the troops came within 150 yards of them, and reserving their fire until they thought themselves sure of the object, discharged a volley, and then fled before the undaunted advance of the 53rd. This regiment then charged a body of rebels, who were drawn up in support of a

---

* The natives almost, if not altogether, worship their guns.

T.

gun, and almost came up with them, but being completely "blown" by the distance they were obliged to run, were unable to get to close quarters with men whose agility is proverbial; the enemy soon made their escape, and succeeded in getting their gun off also. It is in such cases as this that the loss of cavalry has so often been felt; infantry doing all that infantry can do, but being quite unable to do the work of cavalry into the bargain. The siege train in charge of Commander Grant, R.N., kept up close in rear of the line, but had only an opportunity of firing one or two rounds on a village held by a party of the insurgents on our left rear.

In an hour and a half, the rebels being completely routed and driven back, the Ferozpore regiment of Sikhs, a noble corps, pushed on well in front, and were the first (after the rebel army had retired) to enter the fort of Toolseepore, which was found deserted. The rebels, numbering about 300 cavalry, 12,000 infantry, and several guns, came down in three columns, and after having deployed into line, extended to a great distance on the left and right. Sowars were galloping up and down in front of their line, probably encouraging them to exterminate the Feringhees; but their resistance was of short duration, and their cavalry never ventured to charge. One gun was taken by H.M.'s 13th Light Infantry, and one by H.M.'s 53rd, which was left behind when the line advanced, and on returning in search of it, it could not be found. Our force of all arms in the field was about 2,500 men, and our loss was four killed and several wounded, in addition to two or three dhoolee bearers, who were olsa killed. The loss of the enemy could not be easily ascertained, but must have been considerable, many were left on the field, besides many others who, no doubt, were carried off when wounded.

On arriving about 1500 yards from the fort, the siege train halted, and a man was seen on the rampart hoisting something which in the distance looked like a flag. At first those attached to the siege train fancied that their turn had arrived, and were making preparations for action ; but it soon appeared that the man was a Sikh who had entered the fort which the enemy had evacuated in the morning to give battle, and after the defeat thought it wiser not to re-enter. No doubt, as their information was generally better than ours, they heard of the heavy pieces of ordnance that were in the field, and the stalwart men that manned them. Whether the rumour that got afloat among them that seamen were little men, who carried these pieces of artillery under their arm, or not, it is impossible to say ; but from the very absurd stories which were circulated among them by designing men, and which were implicitly believed, when to the prejudice of the Europeans or Government, it may justly be argued that they would believe almost anything.

The fort was constructed in the form of a square, surrounded by a deep ditch, filled with water, and inside the ditch thick mud-walls and bastions; there were houses, a garden and magazine inside, and sufficiently extensive to contain a large force. The powder and arms were destroyed.

Two unhappy accidents occurred in the evening after the action. The troops sat down on the ground to rest, and a private of the 53rd, when taking up his rifle, which he had left on full cock, thoughtlessly held the muzzle towards him, and a twig catching the trigger, caused it to go off, shooting him through the breast. Instantaneous death ensued. And in the evening a soldier of another regiment, under the effects of drink, fired off his rifle through a tent, shooting one Sikh, and wounding another. He was immediately put under arrest to await his trial. It fell to my lot the following morning to commit the remains of the Europeans that fell in action to a soldier's grave.

This was the last action in which the "Pearl's" Naval Brigade took a part, and it was the last general action that took place during the mutiny; the war being declared over on the first day of the new year, in the following week.

The rebels now held no place of any importance, but were scattered about, chiefly on the borders of the jungle skirting Nepaul. After the defeat they retired about six miles, but their position was quite untenable, being hemmed in on all sides, the only outlet being into Nepaul. Our camp, which had been struck and packed in the morning, was sent for and arrived late that evening; much of the baggage, owing to the nature of the ground and the total absence of roads, not coming up until the middle of the night or next day. The troops soon retired to snatch some rest, and prepare for a renewal of the action the following day; but the excessive rains rendering the ground a swamp, caused the movement to be postponed one day more, which brought us to the 25th; and, in spite of it being Christmas-day, all prospects of peace and quietness were banished. After an early breakfast the troops "got under way." A guard was left in the camp, but before marching half-a-mile, intelligence arrived that the rebel force had broken up; their leaders going off in different directions. The troops then returned to camp to prepare the Christmas dinner.

The town of Toolseepore now presented a most desolate appearance; it was burnt the day of the action, and the walls of the houses alone were standing; its streets were rather more regular than usual in native towns, and built in a cruciform shape, one street running at right angles to the other. There were evident signs of the scourge of war in every direction; in one place the ghastly corpse, which lay unburied, and what was still stranger, which had escaped the jackal and the vulture; in another place a pool of water mingled with blood, giving evidence of the resting-place of the slain which had been removed. Here and there miserable-looking mortals might be seen among the ruins, some, perhaps, camp-followers, looking for loot or concealed treasure; others, perhaps, the former owners in disguise, seeking to recover the imperishable metal from the general wreck; and some were wretched, decrepid, attenuated mendicants, to whom the streets may have been a patrimony, but now being left friendless, and having nothing apparently to live for, looked as if it was a matter of perfect indifference how soon they were called upon to die. Such are the sad results of war. Well may it be regarded the heaviest scourge that can befal a nation. It not only renders many a wife a widow, and many a family fatherless, and many a house sad, and many a heart sick; but an invading army carries desolation wherever it goes, marching, perhaps, through richly cultivated land, where the crops of standing corn, which have been cultivated with care, and toil, and expense, are trodden down and destroyed by horses, by elephants, by oxen, by artillery and men; and in addition to this, its tendency to deaden the principles of religion, by often being obliged, in self-defence, to meet the enemy on days held sacred among Christian nations, and by accustoming men to regard life as of little value, and hardening instead of awakening them to a sense that they are beings destined to live for ever.

CHAPTER XIII.

Christmas-day, 1858—March to Pepyreah—Sir Hope Grant's Flying Column—March to Puchpurwah—Naval Brigade ordered to the Ship—The Farewell—Governor-General's Opinion of the Naval Brigade—Dinner given to the Seamen at Calcutta—Dinner given to the Officers at Madras—Voyage Home—Names of Officers.

THE troops had no sooner settled down in camp than Sir Hope Grant arrived, having ridden over in the morning from his own force, which was posted more to the southward; and after a conference held with Brigadier Rowcroft, further intelligence having, in the meantime, arrived, that the rebels were making all speed to get to the eastward along the Tarai,* orders were issued that the force should immediately follow in pursuit. The great object was to

---

* A belt of jungle between British India and Nepaul.

prevent them from escaping in that direction, lest they should again inundate Goruckpore and perhaps Bengal. The Christmas dinner, already in process of preparation, was completely "knocked on the head." The tents were struck, the baggage was packed, and the force started off to the northward, inclining towards the east, to intercept them in their line of march.

H.M.'s 53rd Regiment was left to hold Toolseepore, and prevent any escape in that direction, while the force under Brigadier Rowcroft commenced the march about noon, passing over a country without roads, fording nullahs, and crossing dykes. The baggage-carts were unfortunate in getting into holes, and ruts, and heavy ground. Occasionally one would capsize, and another would stick in a ditch, three feet deep in mud, obstinately obstructing the progress of all the others that followed. The siege train, composed of heavy guns and mortars, drawn by elephants and bullocks, was sometimes in a "regular fix," being completely stuck in the mud; but by patience and perseverance, and no small share of exertion on the part of the seamen and marines, it arrived at the camping-ground in the evening, the last of them being parced about ten o'clock P.M. A strong reconnoitring party, under Lieutenant-Colonel Cox, had been sent out after the enemy early in the day, and came up with their rear-guard; but darkness setting in, it was impossible to pursue further, and he returned to the camp. Very little baggage made its appearance until the following morning, and some unlucky ones did not see their carts for three consecutive days. Fortunately the tents were pitched a little before dark, and those who had no charpoy, retired to rest on a bed of straw scantily supplied, on wet ground. There was not much in the proceedings of the Christmas-day to remind campaigners of the peace and quietness that prevail at this season of the year in favoured lands. There was no reunion of friends, but a hot pursuit of enemies; the bell of the village church was not heard to toll, but the shrill notes of the bugle were frequently sounding; in fact, there was nothing to remind of "home."

The men breakfasted early that morning, and being ordered to strike the camp before dinner was ready, in addition to a wearisome march, they were obliged to fast until late at night. It fared a little better with the officers. The kansama, or head native steward of our mess, no sooner arrived on the camping-ground, than he lit a fire, and then having speared a turkey, a brace of geese, and a brace of fowls on a long iron spit, put them to roast horizontally in front, while a ham and other dinner appurtenances were deposited in their respective pots on the top of it. Having then spread rugs on the ground before a blazing fire, many, after a fatiguing day, lay stretched, getting the benefit of the heat, which was as acceptable as on a cold Christmas night in England. It was a misty, dark, and damp night. But campaigners must rough it and make themselves as comfortable, in spite of appearances, as the circumstances will admit. British officers lying before the fire on one side, and a dozen of kitmutgars on the other, sitting down on their hunkers, shrunken with the nipping cold, formed a picture sufficiently grotesque for *Punch*— the whites *vis à vis* with the blacks, and a blazing wood fire extending longitudinally between them, lighting up their faces and forming a group of whom one party strongly contrasted with the other. After exercising a fair share of patience, at the fashionable hour of half-past ten o'clock, dinner was served up, and in the course of an hour all had retired to snatch a few hours' rest.

Next morning was charming, and the Hymalayas rose to view in all their grandeur. We were not further distant from the nearest spur in the Nepaul territory than fifteen or sixteen miles, and notwithstanding that the highest range was probably sixty or seventy miles distant, their great height and the pure atmosphere caused them to appear comparatively close. But it was not a time to indulge in a reverie on scenery. The rebels were fast getting to the eastward of us, skirting the jungle, and consequently the force marched with as much speed as a country without roads would permit a force to travel, which was encumbered with hackeries for the carriage of baggage and a siege train besides. By sunset we arrived at Pepyrea, and encamped on ground which was almost in every direction a swamp, in consequence of the recent rains. At this season it is more agreeable to march during the day than at three o'clock in the morning, which is usual in India. The cold at that hour is bitter, but during the day the climate is a delightful temperature. The transition from heat to cold in the course of twenty-four hours may be trying to some constitutions, but taking all things into consideration, during the cold season it is very enjoyable.

On the following morning we recrossed the Boora Raptee, marched to Intwa, and pitched the tents on the old camping-ground. Here we found Sir Hope Grant encamped with his flying column, consisting of Hodson's Horse (Punjabees), a troop of Royal Horse Artillery; also the 9th Lancers, who, notwithstanding the rough life, looked in as good condition as if they had just been reviewed in Hyde Park. There were no hackeries drawn by bullocks allowed to march with this column. All the baggage was carried either on ponies or camels, in order that, at any moment, they might be able to go a great distance without impediment or delay. The multitude of camels employed was very great, and the amazing distance these animals can travel with a heavy load, and without food or water, renders them of enormous value in carrying baggage, and constitutes a flying column of great efficiency, at any moment being ready to start off and intercept the enemy when they least expect any opposition. It was by this means Sir Hope Grant was so successful in coming up with the rebels so frequently, and denuding them of such a multitude of guns.

On the 28th there was a halt to refresh man and beast, the cattle not having had an opportunity of being regularly fed for three days; while Sir Hope Grant with his flying column started off towards the north to intercept the rebels in their flight to the eastward. Brigadier Rowcroft's force followed next day, and came up with Sir H.

Grant's encampment at Dhokohuree. No other stronghold being in the possession of the rebels, the siege train was no longer required; it was therefore left behind, and the Naval Brigade were relieved of the labour it incurred in dragging it over such a roadless region.

The light field-guns and rockets were the only artillery that was now manned by the seamen; and they returned to the ranks again to do the duty of light infantry. The men of the Naval Brigade were always on excellent terms with their companions in arms: they seldom were long in camp with any corps without leaving them as friends. Sometimes when a swell trooper commenced poking fun at Jack, he was always ready with his answer, giving as good a piece of humour as he received. Occasionally a little badinage was interchanged about Jack's costume or seat on horseback, which may not have been quite military, not being bestocked to the throat, or so trimly buttoned up to the chin. They were told they might chaff, when they could fire a broadside, or furl a sail in a gale of wind, as well as Jack "handled his guns and galloped his horses on shore." It is no difficult matter to find a Briton inspired by bravery and ready to mount a horse and join in a charge on the enemy's ranks; but it is not every day that men are found who can manage a ship in a tornado, can rig or unrig her if required, can furl her sails in a storm, and weather the most boisterous tempest; and stepping off the plank to *terra firma*, can harness their horses and mount them; can lay down the boarding-pike, and take up the rifle; can make a gun-carriage, a limber and harness, and then come off victorious in upwards of twenty engagements.

On the 29th the force marched to Puchpurwah while Sir H. Grant made a sweep with his cavalry and horse artillery to scour the skirt of the Tarai. He came up with the thieves as they were cooking their dinner, a time when they have a decided objection to be disturbed, and when their "prejudices" are grossly "violated." On the General's approach they bolted into the jungle, which was quite impenetrable to cavalry, and in the evening he arrived in camp. There was a halt at Puchpurwah for some days. We here spent the last day of the year 1858, and on the 1st day of the new year orders were received from the Governor-General that the Naval Brigade should forthwith proceed to Calcutta. The war was declared over. They were well pleased to see the last of it, and, as may easily be imagined, there was a general rejoicing at the prospect of returning home, after serving two campaigns in India.

The three 12-pounder howitzers, ammunition, stores, horses, and ponies were made over to the Royal Horse Artillery, and in the evening of the 2nd of January, Brigadier Rowcroft, C.B., requested permission to address the men before leaving. A parade was ordered for the purpose, and the Brigadier expressed his regret at the Naval Brigade leaving the force under his command; while he said, " The successes we have gained are mainly due to your courage and gallantry. I have also observed the excellent discipline and conduct of your brigade, which reflects great credit on Captain Sotheby and the officers, as well as on yourselves; I therefore regret to lose your services, but am glad that, upon your departure, you are homeward-bound, which you all so much desire."

Three hearty cheers for the Brigadier rent the air, and they were wound up with one cheer more. Next morning the Naval Brigade left Puchpurwah, many of the officers and men, as well as the band of H.M.'s

13th Light Infantry, accompanying them and playing suitable tunes. When they halted to return to the camp, they gave the brigade three cheers, which was heartily returned, not forgetting a cheer for Lieutenant-Colonel Cox, and one for Lord Mark Kerr, the Colonel of the 13th. They then bade farewell to their companions in arms, with whom they had so often served side by side, and turned their face towards home.

On arriving at Dhokohuree, we found the 6th Madras Cavalry, and H.M.'s 73rd Regiment encamped there; and next day proceeded en route for Allahabad, which was reached, by knocking two marches into one every day, on the 15th of January, and the camp was pitched close to the fort. We marched from the north to the south of Oudh, passing through Fyzabad, Ajjuddia, and Sultanpore; places which will ever be famous in Indian history. A line of forts are constructing at intervals along that road, which may serve as places of refuge for Europeans in the event of another revolt. On the 17th the men embarked in the steamer "Benares," and on the 2nd of February arrived at Calcutta.

The high estimation in which the Governor-General held the "'Pearl's" Naval Brigade, was not more distinctly evinced by his repeated refusal to grant permission to return to the ship, notwithstanding the urgent requests that were continually sent to him on the subject, than by a Gazette "extraordinary," which was published by His Excellency's orders, dated

"ALLAHABAD, *Monday, January* 17, 1859,
Military Department.

"No. 653 of 1859.—His Excellency the Viceroy and Governor-General cannot allow the officers and men forming the Naval Brigade of Her Majesty's ship "Pearl" to pass through Allahabad, on their return to their ship, without expressing his acknowledgment of the excellent service which they have rendered to the State. Disembarked on the 12th of September, 1857, they have for fifteen months formed a main part of the small force to which the security of the wide district of Goruckpore, and of the country adjoining it, has been entrusted, and which has held during that time important advanced posts, exposed to constant attack from the strongholds of the rebels.

"The duty has been arduous and harassing, but it has been cheerfully and thoroughly performed, and the discipline of the "Pearl's" Brigade has been admirable. The Gazettes of the 9th and 23rd March, 27th April, 11th May, 22nd June, 6th and 13th July, 13th August, 12th and 19th October, 23rd and 26th November, 1858, and 11th January, 1859, have shown that when the Goruckpore Field Force has been engaged, the brigade has signally distinguished itself.

"The Governor-General cordially thanks Captain Sotheby, C.B., and his brave officers and men, for the valuable assistance which they have given to the army in Bengal, and he is glad to think that they do not quit the scene of their services without the satisfaction of seeing peace restored to the rich districts which they have protected.

"R. J. H. BIRCH, Major-General,
Secretary to the Government of
India with the Governor-
General."

From the very first His Excellency clearly perceived the value of experienced artillery, that arm of the service being proverbially of paramount importance in Indian warfare; and knowing what a great augmentation the brigades of the "Shannon" and "Pearl" would be to the military forces, gladly accepted their services as soon as volunteered, and refused permission to their leaving the country at a time when troops were imperatively demanded to maintain our very existence in India. And thus a practical example was given how the navy can be turned to the best account in a great emergency; that seamen, from their pliability of character and habitual obedience to command, can easily adapt themselves to any circumstances; and, instead of spending their time at cutlass-drill or shifting topsails in a peaceable port by way of exercise, are ready at any moment, when there is no enemy to meet on their own element, to man a battery or take the field, with undaunted bravery in active service, as artillery, five hundred miles from their ships, and thereby render incalculable service to the State.

On the return of the seamen and marines to Calcutta, they were entertained by the inhabitants at a public banquet in the Town Hall, as an expression of their sense of the services they had performed. Calcutta had never witnessed anything of the kind before except once, when the men of the "Shannon," on their return from the North-Western Provinces, were greeted by a similar entertainment. The hall of the building was decorated in a very effective and tasteful manner; on every column were flags, and standards, and streamers, their bright colours mingling with the softer hues of the flowers and evergreens, which hung in graceful festoons. The walls were adorned with transparencies, stars of arms, and other devices. There was much ingenuity displayed to add brilliancy and gracefulness to the decorations; the tables extended the whole length of the hall, in parallel rows; and in the centre was a circular one, around which the petty officers and non-commissioned officers assembled. The Governor-General's band, and also the band of the 99th, were in attendance, enlivening the entertainment by their performances.

About six o'clock the men landed from the ship (two hundred and five in number), and, preceded by the band of the 99th, marched to the Town Hall, where they were loudly cheered by the assembled inhabitants of Calcutta, while the band played " Rule Britannia;" a numerous assemblage of ladies and gentlemen, among whom were some of the highest officials, waiting to receive them ; and nothing could exceed the warmth of their reception ; and nothing could be more cordial or complimentary than the expressions of those who bid them welcome. Among those present and foremost at the hospitable board, were Sir J. Colville, General Sir James Outram, and Mr. Ritchie.

The usual toasts were proposed after dinner by the petty officers and non-commissioned officers of the Royal Marines, and received with almost deafening bursts of cheering. First the Queen; then the Prince Consort and the Royal Family; then his Excellency the Governor-General; and next came Sir James Outram and the army. The gallant General was lavish of his compliments; and in recounting the deeds that had been done by the Naval Brigade, produced them as a proof that "British seamen would never disappoint the expectations of the British people."

After the community of Calcutta and their hospitable entertainers were proposed, and the toast duly honoured, it was responded to by Sir J. Colville, who congratulated the men, after conquering in many arduous struggles, in bringing back their intrepid commander; and pointed out how much more fortunate the "Pearl's" Brigade was in that respect than the Brigade of the "Shannon," to the memory of whose gallant Captain a just tribute of respect and honour was paid. He concluded his speech by proposing the health of Captain Sotheby, which the men received with rapturous cheering.

The petty officers by this time began to gain confidence, and one after another rose up to propose several other toasts, not forgetting their old companions-in-arms up the country, the Bengal Yeomanry Cavalry, Lord Mark Kerr, and Lieutenant-Colonel Cox, and H.M.'s 13th Light Infantry; also Brigadier Rowcroft, who led them on to victory in many an action. And about half-past nine o'clock the dinner party was broken up, and the men separated in an orderly manner, some returning on board the ship, and some preferring to remain on shore for the night.

But, among the many speeches that were made, perhaps a higher compliment was not paid by any than that by Mr. Ritchie, the Advocate-General, who at a public meeting in Calcutta, assembled for the purpose of interesting the inhabitants to support a chaplain for the merchant-seamen, contrasted the general demeanour of the Naval Brigades composed of the seamen of the Royal and Indian navies, with those composed of merchant-seamen, who had not been brought under the restraints or moral training of religion. Speaking of the crews of the "Shannon" and "Pearl," "names that will never be forgotten in Calcutta," he said, "It was not their prowess in the field to which I allude, though this has never been surpassed even by British sailors; but their admirable steadiness, good conduct, and humanity, throughout a most trying campaign, and under circumstances of great temptation." And having given the merchant-seamen full credit for their bravery in the field during the mutinies, contrasted at the same time, the good conduct and discipline of the others, with the demeanour of those against whom charges for several offences had been brought officially before his notice.

On the 13th of February, 1859, the "Pearl" left Calcutta, and called in at Madras, where the officers were as hospitably entertained by the members of the Madras Club, as the men were at Calcutta. The banquet was nobly served, and the rooms were thronged with members who came, at an unavoidably short notice, to receive their guests. This "feast of reason, and genuine flow of soul," went off as such a banquet should go off, indicative of goodwill and kindly feelings on the part of the entertainers and entertained; having met together as strangers, and having parted as friends. The "Pearl" was to sail on the 25th; but the hearty invitation from the members of the club was not to be put off, and consequently there was a delay until the following morning. The services that had been rendered by the Naval Brigades were not unknown at Madras. Their actions were often recounted, and "Peel and Sotheby" were chronicled in the leading journal "as household names."

In thus recording the actions of the past, and giving honour to whom honour is due, it would be unbecoming to pass over in silence the courtesy and consideration shown by the other services, from his Excellency the Governor-General, downwards. That great statesman, with a coolness undaunted by dangers, and with a firmness unshaken by alarms, steered a mighty empire through troubled waters, and brought her to an anchor in peace. And when so-called errors of judgment are hid under the shadow of an increased reputation, history will closely associate his name with some of the grandest achievements in the East.

Although our loss in action was trifling, yet the sum of those who were wounded, who died, or were killed in action, and were invalided in consequence of the effects of exposure or climate, amounted to about one-fourth of the number of men who formed the original force. Most of those who were invalided recovered, as well as the wounded, who were skilfully treated by Mr. J. W. Shone, the surgeon in charge, and whose attention to the sick was at all times unremitting.

It would be difficult to account for the small loss sustained in action, except it happened that the Sepais, like the Gorkhas, (and I have heard the same remark made of other Easterns, with what truth the reader may judge from the results), paid more attention to the distance the balls carried than to the taking of an accurate aim at the object. This may arise from the use of arms that do not kill point-blank at a greater distance than a hundred yards. The Gorkhas serving with the brigade have often been observed to point their muskets in the air and fire away. If the Sepais adopted the same plan, the difficulty would be accounted for. And again, when the rebels took up a position, it was their custom to wait to be attacked. When the attacking force arrived at a spot for which they had their guns laid (the range being known), they discharged a few rounds. Sometimes their fire takes effect; but when the line pushes on, they lose their range, which, from their excitement, they seem never to regain; or, shall we not be willing to acknowledge the providence and protection of a higher Power, who showed a favour unto us by crowning our arms with victory, by shielding our troops from harm, and reserving the great and rich empire of India to the sway of Britain for higher and nobler ends, calling upon us to do something more for that people than has ever yet been done, to give light among the benighted, and diffuse the knowledge of Christianity among nations and tribes who wander in darkness and in the land of the shadow of death?

The "Pearl" on her voyage home remained for several days at Trincomalee, and at the Cape of Good Hope, and touching for one day at St. Helena, on the 6th of June, after an absence of three years and one week, the circuit of the world being completed, the anchor was cast at Spithead. The following day she was ordered into Portsmouth harbour, and on the 16th of June was paid off. The conduct of the men in general was excellent, and punishments were few. The same discipline that prevailed throughout the commission prevailed to the end, and their demeanour during the time of being paid off reflected upon them much credit. The custom of paying-off dinners, which is nearly extinct, was brought to life, and the officers met together in the evening for the last time.

The names of the officers who formed the Naval Brigade were—

Captain Sotheby, who received the order of C.B., and was appointed extra Aide-de-Camp to the Queen.

Lieutenant Pym, Royal Marine Light Infantry.

Lieutenant Turnour, R.N., Lieutenant Radcliffe, R.N., and Lieutenant Grant, R.N., who were promoted to the rank of Commanders for service in the field.

Mr. Ingles, mate, and Mr. Maquay, mate, who were promoted to the rank of Lieutenants, for service in the field.

Lord Charles Scott, who had been invalided in consequence of disease engendered by the climate, during the arduous service of the first campaign.

The Honourable Victor Montague, midshipman, acting Aide-de-Camp to Brigadier Rowcroft.

Mr. Stephenson, midshipman, acting Aide-de-Camp to Captain Sotheby, C.B.

Mr. Foot, midshipman, who was attached to the light field-battery under the command of Commander Turnour.

Lieutenant Fawkes, R.N.

Mr. Edwards, midshipman.

Mr. Merewether, master's-assistant.

Mr. J. Fowler, who was killed in action on the 5th of March, 1858.

Mr. J. W. Shone, assistant-surgeon, who was promoted to the rank of Surgeon.

Mr. Parkin, gunner.

Mr. Cooley, boatswain.

Mr. Burton, carpenter.

Mr. Shearman, assistant-engineer.

Mr. Bowling, clerk.

Rev. Edward A. Williams, M.A., chaplain, R.N.

And thus the services of the brigade were acknowledged by the Lords of the Admiralty, in the promotion of those officers who were eligible for promotion by means of length of service, the lieutenants being made commanders, and the mates lieutenants. The warrant-officers and assistant-engineer were each raised one step in rank; while the petty officers received warrants; and no doubt the midshipmen will be rewarded in due time.

THE END.

www.ingramcontent.com/pod-product-compliance
Lightning Source LLC
Chambersburg PA
CBHW031134160426
43193CB00008B/131